BLOODY MARY

MY STORY

MARY COUGHLAN

HACHETTE
BOOKS
IRELAND

First published in 2009 by Hachette Books Ireland

1

Copyright © 2009 Mary Coughlan

A CIP catalogue record for this title is available from the British Library.

ISBN 9 78 0340 99347 7

Typeset in Sabon by Hachette Books Ireland
Printed and bound in the UK by CPI Mackays, Chatham ME5 8TD

Hachette Books Ireland policy is to use papers that are natural, renewable and recyclable products and made from wood grown in sustainable forests. The logging and manufacturing processes are expected to conform to the environmental regulations of the country of origin.

Hachette Books Ireland
8 Castlecourt Centre
Castleknock
Dublin 15, Ireland
A division of Hachette UK Ltd
338 Euston Road, London NW1 3BH

www.hachette.ie

To my mother and father.

Prologue

30 October 2004

I am sitting in a hearse. Outside the rolled-up windows, the streets of Galway glide by – people walking on the paths, getting on with their own lives, cars going to and from places like any other day – but inside the hearse, it's completely silent and everything is different. The funeral director quietly concentrates on his driving and my mother, who is in the coffin in the back, obviously isn't saying a word. Although I wish to fuck she would.

We're making the journey from Galway Regional Hospital, where my mother passed away a few hours ago, to my parents' home in Claregalway, ten miles away. When her father died, Mammy had this big thing about him being left in the hospital mortuary on his own overnight. But everyone said to her: 'He's dead, he doesn't know any different,' so she just gave in. When she died, I asked my father if he would like Mam to come home for her wake. We asked the priest and he said he didn't think it would be a problem.

And so I find myself riding out with her, in this big black

hearse. It might be silent here, but inside me, there is a storm in full swing. I am fucking livid: so angry, that bitter tears – not tears of sorrow – prick my eyes. I'm raging with my mother for dying, with my husband for betraying me, but mostly with myself for driving him to it, for trying to escape the truth with drugs again, and for being so scared to strike out on my own that I continued to stay with him, despite what he did.

My life has been falling apart, but I've been giving everyone the impression that everything is just great. I'm the recovered alcoholic with the perfect marriage to a man who has loved her enough to stay with her and her children through the terrible times. He's the long-suffering hero who has found his happy-ever-after with the love of his life and, now that she's sober, with a much-publicised dream wedding. Except that it's all a sham, and I'm the one keeping the dream – or the lie – alive.

With my composure intact, inside I'm screaming at my mother in the back of the car: 'You did fuck all for me when you were alive, so now that you're dead, you better fucking help me. Do something! Anything!'

But still the hearse rolls on, the engine like a whisper, the driver staring forward, mouth shut.

In the months leading up to this moment, I literally haven't stopped. My mother's illness; the problems in my marriage; my career; the preparations for my oldest daughter Aoife's wedding: my every waking hour has been filled. So, finding myself quietly being driven across Galway, with my mother peacefully at rest behind me, is allowing me to really think for the first time in ages, and, as my anger dies down, I begin to realise that I am being given a chance. I am making this journey with my mother for a reason.

She and I always had a difficult relationship. I was pretty much the bane of her life when I was younger, causing her no end of grief. But there were reasons for the way I was, things I held her and my father responsible for.

Sometimes as a child, I would plot her murder. The first chance I got, I ran away from home and never came back, not even contacting her to tell her where I was. I told her my deepest, darkest secret – the truth of what happened to me when I was a child – and she told me to shut up, that she didn't believe me. Yet I had found a way in later years to come to terms with her, with us, and before she died, I got to a place where I could tell her I loved her, and feel that love, not just say the words.

Now it was just the two of us together, every word that was said between us had passed and was in the past. And suddenly I knew what I had to do. I could go on holding my mother responsible for the mess I had made of my life forever. I could go on holding responsible everyone else who had hurt me too: my father, my grandfather, my uncles, the men I loved. I could go on feeling guilty for not being a good daughter, for not being a good wife, for not being a good mother, and bury myself in that guilt. I could hold on to the shame, the pain and the anger that had gripped me when I was just a tiny little girl and never, ever went away, and I could try at the same time to shield myself from that guilt, shame, pain and anger by getting drunk, or getting high and losing control.

Or I could just let go.

I begged my mother for help as we rode home in that hearse, and this was her answer: to just let go. The only way I could take myself back into my own hands, the only way I could gain control of my own life after a lifetime out of control, was by letting go.

It sounded so simple, after so many years of searching for answers and for ways to escape. But it wasn't simple at all. In fact, it would turn out to be the hardest thing I had ever had to do. Life had handed me my fair share of horrible shite to deal with, a lot of major ups and terrible downs but, as they say, the bloody worst was yet to come.

1

'Two Little Orphans'

In an article my mother wrote for the *Sunday Tribune* in 1987, she remembers me as: 'a very happy baby, who did all the usual things babies do', but inside the family, the story is a bit less rose-tinted. I may have been the first-born to Peggy and Peter Doherty, but there was a miscarriage before me, which took a lot out of my mother. She was so worried, and superstitious, while she was pregnant with me that she refused to let my father buy a cot or a pram, and would not knit baby clothes herself because, in her own words, she 'didn't dare count her chickens before they were hatched'.

I was born at 6.30 p.m. on 5 May 1956, in a bed in my grandmother's house at 12 Ashe Road, on the Shantalla estate in the city of Galway: a place that would later become the centre of my life.

As no crib had been bought for me, I spent most of the first two days of my life in a dressing table drawer, balanced on two chairs beside my parents' bed. Mammy had her precious little baby girl at last, and everything must have seemed perfect, just the way she liked things to be. But then I started crying. And crying, and crying. My mother couldn't cope with it.

One night, I was bawling my eyes out and she got my father to cycle up to the doctor's. Mammy was at her wits' end. The doctor – Dr Powell was his name – told them to give me a teaspoon of brandy to calm me down. I don't know if it worked, but it's no wonder I turned out a bloody alcoholic, because after that, I was getting a spoonful of brandy every time I opened my mouth to squawk.

Another sure thing that used to work with my crying fits, I'm told, was shoving my pram under the radio on the shelf in the kitchen: the singing would shut me up.

Like most people, my memories of the early years of my life are a hazy jumble of sights and smells, so I have to rely on my mother's recollections, which, as I have mentioned, tended to border on the perfection she was keen to project to the outer world.

Peggy and Peter thought their little Mary did everything – like smiling, sitting up and getting her first tooth – better and earlier than other babies.

I took my first steps on the day my sister Angela was born, five days before my first birthday. When Ma asked my Da if he was disappointed that the second child wasn't a boy, his answer was reportedly: 'If they're all like Mary, I don't mind if we have a dozen girls.'

It's a pity he didn't stay in that frame of mind. My father was great with babies, but as soon as we got older and started to have minds of our own, he wasn't so easy to please.

When I look back on it, I understand that both my parents were products of their time: of a deprived world, an Ireland where life was harsh and unforgiving and people had to struggle against all sorts of odds to make decent lives for themselves. Right and wrong, good and bad, sin and sanctity: all these were as clearly drawn as black and white, with no grey in between. Sexuality and secrets were shoved under the carpet, never to see the proper light of day again.

My father was born and grew up in a house on the edge of a big farm in Burt, County Donegal, near the border. His father worked for the farmer who owned the land, a trade my father was expected to follow too. So, when he was just sixteen years old, he was sent to work on a farm in Omagh.

Listening to his stories of that time, I still find it all hard to believe. He was far away from his family, sleeping on a pile of straw in a barn, with just a threadbare blanket to cover him and rats running about the place at night. He got tea and bread four times a day, and if he was lucky, dinner on a Sunday. Every day of the week there were long, long hours of working the land and tend to the pigs and cattle. The experience certainly toughened him up, though: enough for him to walk away from that life.

Three years later, my father left Omagh for Galway to join the Irish army. It was a huge journey, a new beginning, and he would never fully return to life in Donegal.

He met my mother, Peggy Cooke, at a football match in Galway. Later they met again at a dance. She was wearing a blue dress she had made herself. I know this because three years ago, on the second anniversary of her death, Daddy gave me a photograph of her that had been taken at that dance. It's a black-and-white picture of her, looking as pretty as she was in real life, but my father has had her dress hand-tinted in blue. It's weird-looking, but beautiful. That's how he remembers her, or how he likes to remember her. She never had any faults as far as he's concerned.

I'm not sure what he thought of his own mother, whether he believed she had any faults herself. I know he resented being taken out of school, not having a proper education, and he was always adamant that his own children would be educated. He felt that he would hav progressed more in the army if he had completed his leaving cert.

I know that when my father was an adult, it emerged that his family was not all it seemed: some of his sisters and brothers were actually his half-siblings, and cousins. My grandmother, Maggie, moved in with my grandfather to help rear his five children after his wife, who was also her sister, died young. In time they married and went on to have four children of their own. Later, she also reared one of her own grand-children as her own.

The father I knew couldn't have been further away from that poor little boy who once slept on straw in a rat-infested shed on an Omagh farm. With his jet-black hair, brown eyes and his incredibly handsome face, in his uniform he looked like a glamorous, dashing film star. To me, he was whoever the equiv-alent of George Clooney was back in those days: Cary Grant, maybe. I think he was the only soldier on our road in the suburb of Mervue.

My mother remembered me as a timid child, which,

considering the way I turned out, is a bit hard to believe. 'When we'd have to visit the doctor, how pale and frightened Mary would get,' she wrote. 'She was terrified of injections and would want to cross the road if we passed a clinic where she had had her shots against polio and her three-in-one.'

She also remembers me as 'loving pretty dresses', which is something my mother instilled into her little girls from the start. She was always making clothes. From the outset, myself and Angela were like twins, dressed up to the nines in matching outfits: hers usually pink, mine blue. I used to think mine were blue because the baby my mother miscarried before I was born was a boy. I was supposed to be a boy: that's what I believed, anyway.

Mammy would be very proud when people remarked that we were always beautifully dressed. The clothes she made for us all through the years we were growing up were absolutely amazing. I think that as life became more and more unmanageable for her, this was her way of controlling things, her way of keeping up appearances. We were very alike in that way. Much later, when my own life became unmanageable, I found other ways of controlling things, other ways of keeping up appearances – or at least trying to. It's a pity I didn't turn to dressmaking myself.

As small children, Angela and I would sit and watch Mammy make our dresses. She would be singing away as she sewed. She used to sing all the time: she was mad about music, and loved Pat Boone and Guy Mitchell and Cliff Richard. She had all their singles and their albums, and she would listen to those records a lot as we were growing up.

Both her and my father were huge fans of Bridie Gallagher

– 'The Girl from Donegal' – who had a hit in 1958 with a song called, 'Two Little Orphans'. My mother taught us this song word for word, and one of my earliest memories is of Angela and myself standing on a table in Renmore barracks, singing it for everyone. This was at one of the annual Christmas parties which were given for the children of soldiers. Our red hair had been ringlet-curled in rags the night before, and I was wearing a blue dress with a big white collar, tied in the middle with two little buttons shaped like birds, and black shoes. Angela was wearing a matching dress in red. After singing, I remember being so excited that I was almost hysterical. Of course, the fact that we had gorged ourselves on sweets and red lemonade might have helped with the rush.

I didn't sing on a stage again until I was twenty-eight. When I had my first ever gig in Belfast, Bridie Gallagher sent me flowers. She said she had seen me on television, on Gerry Kelly's show, and liked me. When I called my father and told him, he nearly keeled over with excitement.

For those first few years, we lived in Mervue: myself, Mammy, Daddy and Angela. I don't remember much about the house, except that it had polished pink-and-lavender lino tiles in the hall, on which we used to fly up and down in our socks.

Every single Friday, my father would bring us home a chocolate bar. I can't remember the name of the bar, but it was divided into coloured sections, with pink, orange and lemony stuff inside.

He and my mother didn't drink. On Tuesday nights, a girl from across the road called Mary Crow would come to babysit, and they would go out to the pictures and to Lydon's on Shop

Street for tea and cake afterwards. Mary Crow's claim to fame was that she worked in the Royal Tara china factory. She once made a baby cup and saucer there for Angela and me.

When I was about three years old, Mammy became very ill with suspected TB. She was sent to the fever hospital, where she would spend the next nine months in isolation. As it turned out in fact, my Mammy didn't have TB: she had pleurisy. Meanwhile, we were carted off to live with my grandparents and uncles on my mother's side on the Shantalla estate in Galway.

Every evening, Daddy would cycle down to my granny's house from the Renmore barracks and take me and Angela down to the hospital. He would hold us up on his shoulders so that Mammy could see us, and we could wave at her. That was the only contact we had with her for nine months.

It must have had a terrible effect on her, but my memories of that time are happy. Angela and I played all the time in my granny's house, rolling marbles around in a basin under the table, or playing with the toy trains belonging to my youngest uncles, Kenneth and Gabriel.

Mammy eventually made a full recovery and came home to us, but the separation she had to endure took its toll on her mental health, and she was prone to depression for the rest of her life.

Despite her abiding love for all her children, Ma's depressions would eventually have far-reaching effects, leading my father to behaviour he once wouldn't have thought possible, and a period of pain and sadness in our family that I have struggled to overcome in the years since.

2

'Mary, Mary, Quite Contrary'

As I said, many of my early childhood memories consist of fleeting images and sensations. One of the earliest of these childhood impressions is of being invaded. There is a hand: long, skinny and bony. There is a particular smell. There's a bad, bad feeling. There is a lot of crying. I am lying by myself in my bedroom. The wall is moving; the wardrobe is moving.

I was four when another sister, Carol, was born. Around that time, our family moved from Mervue to Shantalla, to the house next door to my grandparents, where I would live until I would finally be successful in one of my many attempts to run away as a teenager.

With my grandparents lived my mother's brothers Gabriel and Kenneth. I had two other uncles, Desmond and Christy, who came and went a lot during my childhood.

One day my mother brought us out shopping for shoes. We were on our way home. Carol was in the pram and both Angela and I were on either side of it, hanging on to the handle, and we met Uncle Des on the street. I went absolutely hysterical. I threw myself on the ground and started screaming, kicking the buckles off my new shoes. My mother pulled me to my feet at once, telling me to stop the boldness, and we carried on home, but the moment was never forgotten by any of us.

For years and years after that, every time I saw my uncle Des, he would taunt me about kicking the buckles off my shoes in the middle of the street. He took my mother's old chant of the well-known nursery rhyme and made it his own: 'Mary Mary, quite contrary, how does your garden grow?' I used to cringe inside every time he said it, every time he laughed at me. I never forgot that incident or this response and my feelings about him stayed hidden deep inside me so long, and I only wrote a song about it all on my most recent album, fittingly entitled 'Mary, Mary, Quite Contrary'.

I never warmed to my grandparents next door in Shantalla. My granny, Kathleen, my mother's mother, said very little. She had a tight-lip, as if she was always holding something in, not wanting to let it escape from her mouth. Her maiden name was Lally, and she had been sent away from home when she was just twelve years old to work in service in a big house. In reality, it was little more than slavery, and her memories of that time were laced with cold and hunger. It's no wonder then that she fell into the arms of my grandfather, Colman Cooke, when she was seventeen, and became pregnant almost instantly. In truth, she was swapping one hell for another, because throughout his life, my grandfather was a terrible alcoholic with a cruel streak, who doled out beatings to his family whenever the mood took him.

My grandfather's own background wasn't any less deprived. Both his parents died when he was a young boy, leaving all their children to bring themselves up in the wilds of Carna in Connemara. When he was in his early teens, he went to Scotland to make a living picking potatoes and ended up working on the docks. It's there that he most likely picked up his hard-drinking habits. A few years later, when Kathleen got pregnant, he came home. Over the course of their marriage, they had thirteen children, three of whom died of the measles. I don't know if my mother, Peggy, escaped his beatings, but I do know that my uncle Kenneth has dark memories of being beaten by his father from one side of the house to another, and he witnessed the other boys being viciously attacked too.

Apparently while my mother was growing up with her many siblings, her mother would often pierce the chaos with a threat of: 'Wait 'til your father comes home.' It was a threat my own mother would in turn use many times with us.

Granny Cooke was a model of industry, always cooking and baking, always doing something. She used to make bread every single day. She would bake a huge treacle cake for all the family twice a week, and every day she would send one of my uncles into our house to light the fire. And she was the mistress of turning a blind eye to what was happening in her family.

When we moved to Shantalla, Angela and I were sent to St Bridget's school, near the estate. I vividly remember my first day there. Mammy had knit me a blue-and-white striped jumper and I had a huge big bow in my hair.

Ma had us reading and writing before we went to school. I skipped the first class because I was so advanced. I went from high infants into second class. My teacher there was Sister Pious, the nun who made me consider convent life. I got hooked on

Bible stories for a while and on the idea of being as holy as the Virgin Mary herself.

There was a luminous statue of the same Virgin Mary on my parents' dressing table at home and I would make altars with buttercups and primroses bunched into eggcups around it. I would get down on my knees to pray and think that the Virgin's cape was a gorgeous shade of blue. At Lent, myself and Angela gave up sweets. We kept all the bars and jellies my father would bring home for us after work in a big tin in our bedroom, marvelling over how much we had collected, but never touching any of it. One time, however, the temptation became too overwhelming and we decided to just have one thing each. Of course, our mother walked in and caught us, chocolate smeared across our mouths. We were mortally ashamed of ourselves.

My teacher, Sister Pious, was the most beautiful creature I had ever laid eyes on. I fell stone mad in love with her. She had these two huge brown eyes and her wimple was a blinding white. I would have done anything for her. I used to wonder why she was a nun. Why would somebody so beautiful be a nun? And did she have hair underneath that veil? Did she ever take her clothes off? What did she sleep in? Did she just lie down on her back at night still in her full habit and close her eyes, with her hands in the prayer position?

Sister Pious gave us all cards to buy a black baby with. Each card had a circle with a cross in it, and rosary beads attached. Every time you gave a penny for the black babies, Sister Pious would pierce one of the rosary beads with a needle, and when all the beads were pierced, you owned your very own black baby in Africa. We used to give them names, even though I can't remember any of those names now.

I used to imagine the black babies to be like people from the Baluba tribe in the Congo: my father was always going on about them because there was talk of the Irish peacekeeping troops going out there.

You felt safe with Sister Pious. She had a kind of angelic presence. I suppose her kindness and softness provided a sort of sanctuary. I was a child who needed sanctuary. Every summer, we would go and stay with our other grandparents on their farm in Donegal. It must have been in the summer between high babies and going straight into second class that my grandfather sat me on his knee, put his hand into my knickers and his fingers into my vagina, and kissed me, pushing his tongue into my mouth.

I'm not sure if it's the first sexual thing that happened to me, but it was the first thing that happened with him and it was to happen several more times in my early childhood.

The most terrible part of it for me, aside from the awful discomfort and embarrassment, was that I liked this grandfather. He was very old and had kind, twinkly eyes. He carved birds from pieces of wood for me and made shadow puppets on the wall. In my child's mind, I was really confused about how I could like someone and be totally repulsed by at the same time.

In hindsight, with years of therapy under my belt, I can say there was a serious lack of boundaries in the families that came together to make my own. There were so many secrets being hidden on every side, in both my mother's and my father's extended families, that relationships were completely, perversely confused, as were notions of right and wrong. Throughout my childhood, until I learned avoidance techniques around the age of twelve, this confusion would reign supreme in the relationships I had with certain men in the family.

When I eventually ended up getting help many years later, I learned that in that moment with my grandfather, or even earlier, with that unidentifiable hand, I became stuck. I grew up, I became a wife and mother, had a successful career and lived an adult life, but deep inside I was stuck in that moment. It was to that moment that I would return again and again, as I tried to deal with my everyday life and the hurts that came my way, as hurts must come to everyone. I would react like an outraged child every time I was slighted in the smallest way or in the worst way: I couldn't distinguish between big and small hurts. I would become that little girl, sitting on my twinkly-eyed grandfather's knee, loving him and being violated and betrayed by him at the same time, and not understanding what the hell was really going on.

Our family was growing. Gerard was born two years after Carol, and as I grew older, and probably more and more difficult because of the secrets I was carrying around, my mother was less and less able to cope. I began to talk back to her and she wasn't able to handle it. She certainly wasn't able to handle having four children. She still made all our clothes and had us going around dressed up like little dolls; she cooked all our meals as regular as clockwork and made sure we did our homework. But slowly she was beginning to change, to become more and more detached.

Mammy was forever losing things. Her purse, the house keys, little things like that. Once or twice she lost my father's entire pay packet. In the kitchen we had a picture of St Anthony with a little red light on a shelf beneath it. When my mother would lose something, she would put a half-crown on the little shelf and say a prayer for St Anthony's intervention, promising to put the half-crown in the poor box if she found what she was looking for. She claimed it absolutely worked – although when the lost object was found, the half-crown would be pocketed again.

I don't know if St Anthony had anything to do with it, but one day I found a lovely, orange ten shilling note in the house. (To put this in perspective, our rent at the time was seventeen shillings – so it was a fair amount of money.) Off I went with it, down to Dooley's shop at the bottom of Ashe Road. I spent the whole amount on sweets and bags of Perry's crisps, which I then doled out to all the kids on the street.

When my father found out about it, he went marching down to Mrs Dooley and read her the riot act. 'How could you have let her spend ten whole shillings?' he roared at her. 'Where did you think she got that kind of money?'

I can't remember how I was punished for the misdemeanour, so maybe the incident happened before my father had started doling out what we called 'lashings' with his leather belt.

The 'lashings' began, I think, when my mother was pregnant, yet again, with my youngest brother, Martin. I think she plunged into a depression and wasn't able to cope with her three noisy girls, running around like blue-arsed flies, and baby Gerard in need of so much attention. Her sixth pregnancy, with

Martin, was a catalyst for the change that came over our house.

My father would come home from the barracks every evening at about a quarter to four. I remember Mammy outside in the backyard, making herself vomit into the gutter, with her fingers down her throat. Then she'd be crying just before my father walked through the back door. He'd say: 'What's wrong, love?' And she'd say: 'Mary is at it again.' That's all I remember her saying to him when he came home: 'At it again. She's at it again.' Mammy would complain and then Daddy would take his leather belt off and lash me, while Mammy stood in the corner begging him to stop. I think for a long time I was too scared of him, or too in awe of him, to do anything but take my punishment.

I was punished so often as a child that it eventually became meaningless. But there is a very early incident that sticks out from all the others in my memory, the reason being that it was to shape who I was to become in so many ways. I have never, ever been able to get it out of my mind.

I don't know what age I was, maybe four or five. I was sent out to bring in some coal for the fire – I was given little jobs like that. This time, when I left the coal bucket down, it fell over. No matter how much I protested my innocence, I got whacked for it. I remember thinking that it was the most unfair thing that had ever happened. Nobody would believe me. From that point on, I spent a fair bit of my life thinking that nobody believed a word I said, and later I would decide that I would do whatever the fuck I liked, because I was going to get punished for it anyway even if I hadn't done anything.

In those earlier years, maybe the idea that no one believed

me was part of the reason I didn't tell on the uncle who started abusing me – a man who in any case is long dead and buried now. One night when I was in the bath, this uncle walked right into our house, came upstairs and into the bathroom, and started masturbating in front of me. I was just sitting there in the lukewarm water, with my knees up to my chest, my hair dripping wet down my back, not knowing where to look. I knew what he was doing was wrong, and it felt shameful to be there while he was doing it, but this wasn't the uncle I was frightened of: this was an uncle I looked up to and loved, who was a great influence on me then and for several years to come.

I didn't stop him. I didn't tell anyone. I somehow felt to blame, that it was my fault he was doing what he was doing. And just like it was with my grandfather, I couldn't reconcile the fact that he was doing this horrible, repulsive thing with the fact that I loved him. I know now that this is when my real anger began to take root.

At home, my mother was sick all the time, still complaining on and on to my father about Mary being 'at it again'. Sickness, or 'her nerves' as she used to call it, grew to be a lifetime excuse for escaping from reality, for giving up responsibility. When Mammy was 'sick', Daddy was always there with his belt, doling out some punishment or other and telling me it was for my own good.

I know now from talking to girls who were in school with me that in those days nearly everybody was being brutalised at home. But different people cope with things in different ways. I coped with what was happening to me by finding my own

26

ways to escape, which I would continue to take refuge in for much of my life to come.

The first escape route was out on to the road. Ashe Road, that is. Sometimes now, when I can't sleep, I mentally go through all the people I remember from Shantalla, naming the families that lived in each house and counting how many children they each had. The Sullivans had thirteen, the McDonaghs had fourteen, the Connolly had seventeen, the Connollys next door to these Connollys, had twenty-one. Mrs Reed had twenty-five live children, the Wynnes had ten, the Nallys had eight. There were some families who only had two kids, but they were few and far between. The minute the school bell would go at St Bridget's, all the kids from Ashe Road would be tearing out the door like lightning to get home, as they'd get the first sitting at dinner if they got to the table quick enough.

If inside my house, my thoughts were turning to darkness, outside on the street, life was pure bliss. We were this big, messy gang of children, always finding ways to enjoy ourselves, even though none of us had anything.

We played skipping and two-balls and a wall, statues and hide-and-go-seek. When the Galway Races were on, we used to put these big ropes across the street and pretend we were the horses galloping to the finish line. Racing milk bottle caps in the puddles was big with us for a while too. There would be all differently coloured foil milk bottle tops: red ones and green ones, gold and silver. We would put a piece of chewing gum on to them and stick a match into the gum, with a piece of paper to make a sail. Then we would set them off against each other in the gully.

One of my good friends was called Mary Walsh, and she and I were forever playing with our dolls together. Mary loved brushing her dolls' hair, and taking care of them, but I was very cruel to mine, sticking needles and pencils into their private parts. The kind of playing that I did with those dolls would send a social worker screaming to the courts nowadays. My friends must have thought I was fucking batty.

There was a little hill at the top of the road, and in the wintertime we'd pour water down it and wait until it froze. Then we'd sit in a basin and go sliding down at a hundred miles an hour. 'Get off the ice, Johnny Joyce,' we used to shout. 'Off the ice, Johnny Joyce!' I was as happy as a pig in shite outside with the gang: my friends, the cousins Susan and Anne Lally, Mary Walsh, Anne Barden, Catherine Devaney, Bernadette Holland and Patricia Wynne, finding all sorts of ways to have the craic.

We would all congregate at a place we called the 'Sliding Rock', or another place called 'The Nook', which was a funny little hideaway, just a kind of cranny in the wall. I think it was there for a water hydrant that was never put in. We all used to sit there for hour upon hour.

On Saturdays, Angela and I would go to Irish dancing lessons, first with Helen Spellman and later with my mother's cousin Peggy Carthy, on Dominic Street. Peggy still has her school of style and deportment there to this day. She was an absolutely stunning woman. She had the hair all bouffant and flicked out like Jackie Kennedy, and orangey-red lipstick. She was like a stick insect and when she walked, she carried herself straight as a pole, with her chin in the air. Her style of teaching was old-fashioned to the core, stern and strict and all about keeping your upper body as rigid as a corpse while your legs kicked as high into the air as was humanly possible. It was murder on the dance floor and we loved and dreaded it all at the same time.

One of the boys in our class was called Michael Cazabon. He was black, which was very exotic to us back then, and he was a great Irish dancer, the best in the class. Michael was chosen to go to Dijon in France to represent Ireland in a dance festival.

He still tells the funny story of dancing at a show in the Great Southern Hotel Galway for American tourists. Afterwards a member of the audience came up to him and congratulated him, handing him a twenty dollar note. The man described how, because of the strong ultra-violet stage light, all he could see was the dazzling whites of his eyes and bright smile leaping around the stage, as he jumped high in the air as if he might take off at any moment. We have a laugh about that to this day.

We didn't get to dance in Dijon, but we did get to go to the Feis in Athlone, which was just as good. It was the first time we had been away from home and myself and Angela were mad with excitement. I remember the crush and the smell of Tayto crisps in the hall; girls everywhere in hairdos, practicing their steps; all the embroidered dresses.

I can still remember my hair bouncing up and down when I was dancing. I loved the performance of it, even if I hated the learning part. It was all very strict. No smiling, arms straight, jumping high. Our mother embroidered our costumes, of course. I remember one time she embroidered this Olympic flag on my dress. I couldn't make any sense of it at the time: maybe it was something to do with Ronnie Delany's Olympic gold medal the year I was born.

Mammy was still making clothes, still curling our hair, still presenting her perfect little girls to the world. But behind closed doors, things were going from bad to worse.

Looking back, I think that she was actually suffering from severe depression. I remember a lot of crying at night from their bedroom, and Daddy going off in the middle of the night and getting the doctor. So, I guess she had some sort of a breakdown, although we were so young it was hard to understand what was really going on.

The truth is that my mother was really fucked-up for some reason that was never spoken of in her lifetime. When she died, my father used to try and make sense of it all. After her funeral, he said: 'I know she left me something to explain it. I know she left me a letter.' The poor man looked all over the house for this imaginary letter that he knew was waiting for him, a letter which would give some indication of what had happened to make her the way she was. He never found anything.

There was a lot of crying up in my bedroom too, and plotting as well. Because my father was in the army, he had a rifle, and there was much in the way of fantasising about shooting the two of them, or using the hatchet on them. I would plan their murders regularly. I was so angry, I wanted to kill them.

My father built a garage onto the side of the house. That garage was the pride and joy of his life. One day he started digging a hole in the ground inside it. Every evening when he came home from work, he'd go in there and close the door behind him. He'd be digging, and digging, and digging, and digging. I was full sure that he was going to kill our mother and put her in there. You could stand up in this hole, in the end. It was six or seven foot long, six or seven foot deep and I was waiting to see if Mammy was going in. He kept it covered over with an old shed door. Eventually, we found out it was for changing the oil in his car and doing his own mechanics. He had made a pit.

For all the punishments my father gave me, I thought he was amazing – which left me in a constant state of confusion about my feelings for him. This was the same man who would come upstairs when we had been put to bed with cocoa and biscuits – Marietta or custard creams – and kiss me goodnight, after he had lashed me earlier on that evening. This was the man who used to bring me and my sisters up to the barracks every Saturday afternoon, to take us 'out from under your mother's feet'. We knew everyone up at the barracks and we were allowed complete freedom to run around, having a great time.

Our favourite thing at the barracks was to collect empty shells down at the firing range. My Dad was the number one marksman in the army and I was so proud of him, I could have almost burst. I would polish the big, beautiful buckles on his boots and the brass buttons on his uniform, and his big belt with the buckle on it. I used to just love him all dressed up. He was like a film star hero to me.

But this same hero would beat me so badly that I would have to wear long woollen stockings to hide the welts on my legs.

It was so confusing. How could the man I hero-worshipped be so horrible at the same time? Yet there was one important difference about this confusion I had over the two faces of my father. Whereas I felt culpable and ashamed of myself for what happened with my grandfather and uncle, I did not feel guilty when my father punished me. I was absolutely, one hundred percent sure that he was in the wrong, and as time went on I began to hate him more and more.

We got a break from the dire bloody routine of it all when my mother's only sister, Vera, visited from America. Vera had gone to America when she was just sixteen, and it broke my mother's heart. She got a job with a family as a kind of live-in nanny. My mother used to write these massive ten- or fifteen-page letters to her every month, and the same would come back. And every year we would get a box filled with the most gorgeous clothes, stuff you could never imagine getting in Galway. Hats and dresses for me and Angela: a big blue straw hat with flowers, a lime-green dress with boxed pleats for me; a primrose yellow dress for Angela, and a matching yellow hat. One year there was a fur-lined beige duffel coat with leather and bone toggles. It was a boy's coat and the most exotic thing I had ever seen in my life. I got my hands on it and wore it until it had to be cut off me.

Vera got married in America, and had children: our cousins, Jackie, Jim and Brian. But in all those years we never met her husband, Jim. There was lots of wondering about whatever happened to him, whether he was six feet under. He's alive and well today, still with Vera. But he never, ever came home to Ireland with her. At the time it was hugely expensive for a whole family to travel from America, so I figure it was probably down to finances. Though if this was the case, it wasn't mentioned at all.

The three of us girls had to have frocks made for Vera coming home. Both houses – ours and my granny's – were cleaned from top to bottom and painted inside and out. Vera came for a month in with her children. Our cousin Jackie, who was a little older than Angela and I, was like something out of a movie: a gorgeous American kid with a big white smile. We were a bit jealous of her, particularly of her lovely clothes.

I don't remember us ever talking about Mammy's pregnancy with Martin. It wasn't something we knew anything about: the babies just arrived. I do have a strong recollection of my mother wearing a massive blue frock, standing at the ironing board, talking to her friend, Bernie Ray. They were saying something about it 'coming in her back', which must have meant she was getting back pain. And then this long, skinny baby just appeared in our lives, with his little knitted yellow suits and wee blue bootie socks.

There was another baby, about a year after Martin: a little girl called Valerie. But Valerie never came home from the hospital. There was a funeral for her, and in my mind's eye, I can see Daddy with the little white coffin in the back of our pale blue Opel Kadett station wagon, taking her to the place in the graveyard where Mammy is buried with her now.

This was the straw that broke the back of my mother's sanity at the time. It was after Valerie died that Ma went into the psychiatric unit and was gone from our lives for another while. When she came out, she talked about that baby all the time, and she never, ever stopped crying for her. We needed our mother, but the child she lost was the one she spent most of her time thinking about.

And all through these years, my uncle came into the house when no one was around and masturbated in front of me. Things were progressing a little and he was beginning to fondle me too, touching me here and there. And the more he touched me, the more I began to blame myself for what was happening.

3

'The Sound of Music'

By the time I was ready to make my first Holy Communion, I had the fear of God in me. I thought that when I went up to receive the body of Christ, I'd be struck down there and then, and sent to hell. Because of what was happening with my uncle and grandfather, I thought the mark of sin staining my soul was so dirty that, although nobody knew what was happening, everyone could see that I was a bad girl. A rotten girl.

The night before my Communion, I lay in the bath, trying to think of some way that I could avoid having to do it. What if I fell and broke my arm? That might get me out of it. I started throwing myself down in the bath, trying to break my wrist. But I wasn't very successful, or maybe I was too scared to try hard enough.

When it came to it, I wasn't struck down, of course. Instead, I thoroughly enjoyed my Communion Day. My mother made my dress, a beautifully shaped, intricate thing, and I thought I was the bee's knees in it. There was a huge big party up in the school after the Mass, with Sister Pious there, and Sister

Catherine and Mother Magdalene, whom I also liked. The nuns had all the classrooms done up with tablecloths on the desks, and there was lemonade and millions of sweets.

My father grew peony roses just for the May Procession a couple of weeks later, when all the first Holy Communion children walked through Galway, the girls in their white veils, strewing petals on the streets. We had this basket at home: I think it was made of brass, although at the time I believed it was solid gold. Mammy lined it with lace and Daddy filled it up with the flowers. For the Procession, I had more roses than anybody else, and although my feet were killing me by the end of it, I got a great kick out of tossing the petals from my golden basket.

The summer after my Communion, the family went, as we had done every summer since I was five, to my grandparents' house in Donegal, on the edge of the big farm in Burt.

My brothers and sisters and I, my uncle Kenneth from Galway, who was the same age as us, and loads of our cousins from all over Donegal and Scotland, spent those summers running wild outside, free to roam wherever we liked. We were always on the go. Sometimes to the stream nearby to catch tadpoles, sometimes across the fields to the shores of the Swilly. Or we'd run next door to see Willie Ramsey, who was a Protestant and had a glass eye, which he'd take out to show us. And every so often, my grandmother would take us on the bus into Derry.

She would pull on her high-waisted coat, above the crossover apron she always wore, put her hair up in a bun and plant a kind of beret-like hat on top of it, and we'd be off. Derry was a big city to us, a big city in a different country. As time went on, it would become more and more different. I remember, towards the last of my visits to Donegal, whenever the British soldiers came, seeing all the barbed wire which had suddenly sprung up, and not knowing what was happening. On the way home from Derry on the bus, we heard stories about the women in the city throwing eggs over the barbed wire at the soldiers. It was hard to understand what was actually going on, but we thought it was great fun altogether.

After we returned home to Galway that summer, we bought toy guns and helmets in Woolworths, and for a while we played at defending the house from the Brits. We would be up on the roof, with our guns cocked.

My grandmother came home from Derry with a different purchase, if she purchased it at all. From beneath her coat and the two huge pockets in her apron, emerged two pounds of butter. She was a law unto herself, really.

Angela and I were the only ones in the family with the same healthy head of red hair as my grandmother in Donegal, and we felt special because of it. I think I inherited her constitution too, her physical strength and sturdiness. I can picture her as if it was only yesterday, walking across the back yard, chickens clucking away at her feet, heavy buckets of water dangling from each arm.

Often, if she had to go into Derry, Granny would walk up the lane about a mile and half to the main road and hitch a lift with the soldiers in their Land Rovers. People would be worried for her, that she might be thought of as fraternising with the enemy, but she would have taken a lift from anyone.

When I look back on it, she was a bit strange, really. In her later years, she definitely got a bit funny. She'd take off and go wandering the roads and no one would be able to find her. Sometimes I get worried I might end up the same way.

I suppose much of my time during those summers in Donegal was spent escaping too, out into the wilds. After the first few summers, I learned to steer well clear of my grandfather, who would always be in the house, sitting by the range in his cap, with a big, thick mug of black tea, whittling away on his sticks with a penknife. When he eventually died of stomach cancer, it was said that the black tea had killed him.

Around this time, I also discovered that I could escape into books, particularly Enid Blyton books. I read them voraciously, shutting out the confusing world around me, as I discovered, with Julian, Dick, George, Anne and Timmy the dog, secret passages and smugglers' spoils hidden on faraway islands. Or later, as I was approaching my teenage years, I would have midnight feasts with Darrell and Sally and their friends at Malory Towers, or play all sorts of tricks on the teachers with the twins at St Clare's.

I was very friendly with Mary Heffernan, who was my mother's cousin and lived in Castlebar. We were around the same age as each other, and when the film *The Sound of Music* came to Galway, Mary travelled down on the bus to see it with me. The two of us went to see it every week after that for as long as it was running, which seemed like forever. Watching *The Sound of Music* was like perfect bliss, absolute and total escapism. Although she didn't look like her, to me, Maria was like Sister Pious, only she was a nun who didn't have to be a nun anymore, but could become a mother to some lonely children and bring happiness to their lives.

For a couple of hours, *The Sound of Music* made me believe that this could actually happen, that somebody like this could come into your life. You'd have a hard life one minute, and then the next, you'd have this great fucking life, because of this person.

And the singing! Mary and I knew every word of every song, and I was constantly belting out 'My Favourite Things', or 'Sixteen Going on Seventeen' or 'So Long, Farewell'.

Although those kinds of song are hardly part of my repertoire now, I think with *The Sound of Music* I began to recognise that music could have a deep effect on me. We had always sung, we knew hundreds of songs, but before *The Sound of Music*, we were just singing with my mother. I didn't really attach anything to it.

Mammy would start singing the minute she got into the car beside my father. She never drove. She tried to a few times, but the car would bump and jump along the road, they'd have a huge row and she'd start crying. The next minute, she'd be singing again. All those mad songs she loved: 'Itsy Bitsy, Teenie Weenie, Yellow Polka Dot Bikini', 'She Wears Red Feathers and a Hula-Hula Skirt', or anything by Guy Mitchell, who all us girls thought was only feckin' gorgeous, 'Singing the Blues', or Pat Boone's 'Love Letters in the Sand': these were big favourites.

The singing stopped for a while when, at the age of two, my brother Martin suddenly got very sick. They sent for the doctor: Dr Fogarty was her name. I remember her bundling Martin up in a blanket, and throwing him into the back of her own car, driving him down Ashe Road to the hospital like a bat out of hell, with Mammy and Daddy racing in their car behind her. As usual, we were left at Granny's.

It seemed like forever that they were down at the hospital. They didn't come home that first night. As we were told later, they had to put Martin into a big bath of ice cubes to bring down his temperature. He had meningitis.

Dr Fogarty was charged with saving his life. He was in the baby unit in the hospital, and Mammy and Daddy were down there all the time with him. The first time I ever saw my father cry was when he came home one of those nights. He was sitting at the kitchen table, just bawling and bawling and bawling, and we thought Martin was dead.

But Martin is a survivor by nature. My mother was very protective of him when he came out of hospital, and I think I started to take more notice of him too. He was a really pale baby, absolutely gorgeous with these big china-blue eyes and huge sausage curls. Mammy loved those curls.

I had no ambition to have babies when I grew up: I wanted to be something much more glamorous than a wife and mother – a fashion designer. I had a doll called Tressy, and when you pushed a button on her stomach, her hair grew. If you turned a coin in her back, the hair shrank again. I loved this doll to bits and I took to designing clothes for her, one-piece creations with huge collars. I was big into collars and puffy sleeves. I would write to my cousin Maura in New Zealand every month about my designing ambitions. She's kept a lot of the letters and they have pictures of the dresses that I designed for Tressy.

At another stage, I decided I would be an artist. An awful lot of painting went on in our house. We were constantly making pictures, using our little boxes of watercolour paints, with all the different coloured squares in them turning muddy brown as we concentrated on our efforts. Mammy, despite her difficulties, was a very creative woman, and she encouraged that side of us without question. It probably kept us busy too and out of her hair, which was no bad thing.

By the time I was ten, I was already developing breasts and filling out. I looked much older than I was. I had this lemon-yellow and lime green dress that my mother made, which I loved. It had an empire line that, I suppose, enhanced my tiny boobs. I wondered was it the fault of the dress that my uncle would want to feel me up. He would just launch himself at me and there would be all this feeling and fondling of my body, while I did nothing, just went blank. But I didn't stop him. I suppose I didn't know how to stop him, but because I didn't, I still felt responsible for it. If it wasn't the green and yellow dress that was making him do it, it must have been me.

In all the years that I was sexually abused as a child, I was never raped. But this had its own problems attached to it. As I grew up into puberty and adulthood, because I wasn't raped, I dismissed the idea that I had been abused. I had been fondled and felt, kissed and probed, had watched my uncle do unspeakable things, but I dismissed it for a long time as something less than abuse, something I couldn't feel sorry for myself about.

The first time I ever spoke to a counsellor about it, many, many years later, I said: 'Look, it wasn't that bad.' And she said: 'What do you mean, it wasn't that bad? When you were five, your grandfather stuck his tongue down your throat and put his fingers inside you. All through your childhood, your uncle masturbated in front of you, and touched you in a way that no child should ever be touched. That is sexual abuse. You were a sexually abused child.'

One way or another, when it was happening, I blanked it out. I tried to avoid it as much as I could, but when it happened, I just went numb. And I found more ways to escape.

Music first really began to have an effect on me with Julie Andrews running around the hills of Austria, but soon my influences began to expand. At the centre of this exploration into a new world of music were my uncles Gabriel and Kenneth, who each had their own definite tastes. Kenneth was a Beatles freak and Gay was an Elvis fanatic. They had a record player, and thousands of records between them. Gay must have had every single and album Elvis released, all kept pristinely in their covers, the dark blue Decca label in the middle of them. He was in the Elvis fan club and he would go off on his bicycle to see this other Elvis nut, Kevin Brophy, down the road, with boxes of records balanced on the carrier, for the two of them to listen to together.

In 1967, Kenneth queued up all night at Raftery's shop to get the Beatles' *Sgt Pepper's Lonely Hearts Club Band* album. When he brought it home, we were all enthralled with it. Inside there was this dressing-up kit, with little paper glasses and everything. Earlier on, when I was about nine, Kenneth had introduced me to the Beatles' *Rubber Soul* album.

The first time I ever saw *Top of the Pops* was in my grand-parents' house in Donegal, and it had a profound effect on me. My grandmother made me a big mug of hot chocolate and I sat, entranced by the likes of The Move singing 'Blackberry Way', transported to a different world altogether. This was during my last ever visit to the farm in Burt. The following summer I refused to go.

I also refused at first to go on the great, epic family holiday of 1968. It had long been my father's big ambition to take the whole family on a tour in the car from Galway all around the entire coast of Ireland. A round trip, you might call it.

I was twelve at the time, and I was very grown-up for my age. I was absolutely adamant that I wasn't going. But with my father, you couldn't be adamant about anything. We were living by 'the Gospel according to Peter Doherty', in which the chief commandment was: 'Thou shalt be a good girl and do what you're told, or else you'll get the living daylights beaten out of you.' So I had no choice, I had to go. But I did so on major sufferance.

As we set out in the blue Opel Kadett, which was packed within an inch of its life with children and suitcases, I took a vow of silence, and refused to open my mouth again for the entire trip. We went down through Limerick, Kerry and Cork, staying in bed-and-breakfasts along the way, with my mother breaking into song in the front of the car every now and then to break the tedium and tension. I didn't sing along. I kept my mouth firmly shut.

One night we got lost. The fog was a pea soup one, so bad you couldn't see the nose in front of your face, and Dad was leaning forward in the driving seat, trying to spot a B & B. The tension mounted and mounted in the car, and in the end they were all shouting and screaming, me with a big puss on my face and the other four kids bawling and hysterical, my mother too. So Dad just pulled up on the side of the road and we stayed there for the night.

In the morning, when we woke up, there were seagulls everywhere. 'Jaysus, we're beside the sea,' I thought, as the windows all fogged up. But we weren't. We all jumped out of the car to find we were on the edge of the fucking dump in New Ross. I will never forget the stink of it and the cursing of my father as we drove away. With my vow of silence still going on, I didn't utter a word of complaint – didn't even crack a hint of a smile.

I melted the day we got to Glendalough. I couldn't stay angry anymore: it was just so beautiful. There's a picture of us all standing beside the edge of the lake, and it's one of my favourite photographs from when I was growing up. There's a kind of serenity to it that I wish my family really had: a moment of pure happiness. They were probably all relieved that I was talking again.

God love him, my poor father. Taking his whole family on that huge trip, and me treating him like shit. I was an awful bitch, when I think back on it. I was twelve, but I thought I was seventeen.

We took a detour up north to Armagh because Dad insisted that he wanted to meet the Archbishop of the city, Cardinal Conway, who was very outspoken about the growing troubles in Northern Ireland. We took pictures of ourselves on the steps of Armagh Cathedral, and then Daddy went off looking for the man himself. He got talking to a housekeeper, but that's as near to the Cardinal as he ever got.

And on we went, over the top of the country to Derry, back down to my other Granny's house in Donegal, for a few days' stop-off before making the final leg back to Galway.

That was my last holiday with the family. The following summer I got a job in a supermarket in Galway called the GTM. I had asked my Uncle Kenneth, who worked there, to get me in. Daddy was planning the annual trip to Donegal, and I knew the only way of getting out of it, of getting out of having to see my grandfather, was to get a job. I stacked shelves and packed bags. Having a job, with the rest of the family off in Donegal, and looking forward to going to secondary school in September, I felt supremely independent and grown-up. I'd even had my first kiss.

Tim Sullivan lived at the top of the road and, Jesus, I thought that this was it. He gave me a peck on the lips and suddenly we were 'going out'. Tim Sullivan. I would go on about him incessantly to my girlfriends. I was in love with him, and thought it would last forever and ever. It probably lasted about three days.

From the moment I hit adolescence, I was mad in the head about boys. Too mad about them, I suppose, because boys would prove to be the key to my downfall and much suffering. They were the reason my father nearly went out of his mind when I was a teenager, the reason I turned my back on both my parents in the end.

A lot of children who are abused end up being really promiscuous as teenagers, and although that did happen to me in my late teens, in the earlier part of my adolescence, it was all very innocent. But I don't think my parents, particularly my father, saw it that way. From the age of ten, I looked and acted a lot more grown-up than my contemporaries, and I think my parents were scared shitless that I was going to get pregnant or something, that I would be up to all sorts of no good.

It's a pity they didn't look closer to home. I don't know when the last time my uncle abused me was. I can't remember a moment when it stopped. I was probably getting too independent and strong-minded to be messed with like that. I had learned to avoid him and learned to avoid that part of myself that had been abused by him and by my grandfather. I would not think about it again for years, but it was always there, always underpinning my every move, and as my teenage years would progress, I would find ever more extreme ways to escape the truth about myself and my family.

Many years later, in my darkest hours, I would curse myself for not speaking up, for not saying anything to my parents. But in reality, it was more powerful than me.

One thing was for sure: no matter what I said, they wouldn't have believed me.

4

'I'll Be Your Baby Tonight'

I was only in the door of secondary school when I started
making a name for myself. And it began with my socks.

We went to the Presentation Convent, Angela and I, or 'the
Pres' as it was called in Galway: an all-girls school. The boys'
school, St Joseph's, or 'the Bish', was up the road. Our uniform
was a horrific royal blue thing: sweaters and skirts over white
shirts and knee-high white socks. I don't know where the
notion came from, but I started dying my socks. Yellow, green,
purple – anything but fucking white.

In the morning, I would leave the house in my white socks,
with my dyed socks in my bag, and on the way to school, I'd
stop, sit down on the side of the road, take off my shoes and
swap pairs. Then I'd be sent home from school to change my
socks, and I'd do the same thing again, only with a different-
coloured pair of dyed socks in my bag when I left the house to
go back to school the second time.

It was a simple, if slightly weird, act of rebellion, but it was
enough to earn me a reputation that would last until I was

kicked out of the Pres three years later. Not that I was in the slightest bit worried about my name being muck. By the time I hit secondary school, my philosophy of life had blossomed into: 'You're going to get killed anyway, so you might as well do whatever the fuck you like, and then get killed.'

Despite my sartorial rebellion, there were some teachers in that first year at the Pres who liked me and had a lasting influence. We had one called Rosie, who taught us maths and Latin. We were only allowed to call her by her first name, so now I have no memory of her surname. A big, dark-haired woman with a hearty laugh, Rosie had lived in Africa for years. She stood out a mile in that environment, where everyone was just trying to be good and keep their heads down. Rosie was a right-on woman, very broadminded, and she talked to us about things that were to stay with me for years. If I knew her now I'd say we'd be firm friends.

Another teacher who took an interest in me was Tess Brown, who taught French and business studies. For a short while I found it very exotic to be studying French and Latin, English poetry, maths instead of sums, so despite the reputation I was building up, I was good at the schoolwork.

I hated one of the teachers, and maybe because I was such a cheeky little bitch to her, she grew to hate me too. One day I said something – I can't remember exactly what – and she laid into me so hard, it caused a scandal at the school. She battered me so badly that I slid off the chair and down on to the ground under my desk.

My uncle Gabriel, who was teaching there at the time, was in the staff room when this teacher came in at break time and said: 'I really gave it to that Doherty one this morning.'

Somebody asked why. 'The little brat was cheeking me,' she said, 'and I hit her a good thump.' Gabriel said: 'That's my niece you're talking about,' which shut her up, I'd say.

He went to the headmistress, and there was a bit of a to-do about it. The teacher in question left at the end of the year, and the rumour among us all was that she had been fired.

One day I noticed some blood in my knickers. I didn't say a word to anyone because, putting two and two together and coming up with five, I put it down to what my grandfather had done to me.

It happened again a month later, and this time there was more blood. I got a bit freaked out, so I went to the office of the headmistress, Sister Columbia.

'Go home to your mother,' the Sister said, which freaked me out even more. Even in the worst circumstances, you never got sent home from school, so I thought, this is it: I must be on my way out.

Mammy was more practical. She sent me to the bathroom to clean up, and when I came out she gave me a bundle of sanitary towels, a belt to hold them in place and a book called *What Girls Should Know*, by Angela McNamara.

'You are not to speak a word about this to anyone, do you hear me?' Mammy said. 'And when everyone is asleep at night, you can bring those used towels down and burn them in the range.'

All through this time, I kept my job at weekends and holidays at the GTM, where my Uncle Kenneth was still working. I was really proud of myself with my little job. On

Fridays, I would pick up my pay packet at the GTM and go to Anthony Ryan's shop next door to buy a piece of material, and that evening Mammy would help me make a dress, from start to finish. I remember this one beautiful purple dress I made, with leg of mutton sleeves. I had my own sense of the way I wanted to look, even back then.

One of the first records I owned was a single my mother bought for me on the way home from a Donegal holiday I hadn't gone on: 'Love Grows Where My Rosemary Goes' by Edison Lighthouse. I played that single so many times, I'd say the vinyl lost its grooves. From then on, along with pieces of material, I started buying my own singles with my earnings from the GTM. 'Lily the Pink' by The Scaffold; 'Honey' by Bobby Goldsboro; 'Darling Be Home Soon' by The Lovin' Spoonful. For ages, my favourite single was Peter Sarstedt's 'Where Do You Go To My Lovely?'

I was a bit of a ringleader in the gang we had at school, which was made up of Susan and Anne, Catherine, Mary, Patricia, all the girls who had been my constant companions throughout childhood in Shantalla, and my new friend, Tessie O'Gorman. Children from our neck of the woods were expected to be brats. Shantalla was like the Tallaght or Finglas of Galway: a big corporation estate of working-class families. They were mostly good, respectable people doing their best with what little they had, but once you were from Shantalla, you were branded.

My friends and I didn't give a fiddler's fuck what anyone thought of us. Every evening after school, the four of us would tuck our uniform skirts up around our tummies under our jumpers to make them into mini-skirts, and we'd walk into town, past the Bish, showing off our legs to attract attention from the boys. I'd be swishing my red hair about too, trying to look as alluring as possible.

Regularly, when we would be walking into town on Prospect Hill, there would be girls, accompanied by nuns, walking on the other side of the street. These, Susan and Anne told me, were girls from the Magdalen Laundry. 'They're all prossies,' added Tessie, who lived near the laundry. 'They get preggers and the nuns take them in.'

This was the first time I ever heard of unmarried mothers. I didn't know what a prostitute was. The most shocking thing I knew was that Catherine Devaney's older sister Mary had a bikini hidden in her suitcase and she was going away on holidays with her boyfriend. We snuck into her room, opened the case and tried the bikini on. Catherine and I practiced kissing an apple and the dressing table mirror to see what it would be like for Mary and her boyfriend.

For years, that's what we thought the Magdalen girls were: pregnant prostitutes taken in by the nuns. It makes me sad to look back on those miserable young ones, heads down, policed by hard nuns dressed in big black habits. Some of these girls were the victims of rape and incest, all sorts of horrible things, and there we were on the other side of the street, carefree, with our skirts rolled up around our waists to catch the eyes of the boys. If you think about it, there was only a hair's breadth between me and that laundry.

*

The first time I ever had a drink was at the annual GTM Christmas party. I was thirteen. I got drunk on Babycham, the bubbles going to my head in an instant. I'm not sure if I liked the taste or the feeling, but I felt very grown-up, which was my big ambition in those days, and I remember roaring with laughter at almost anything anyone said.

When we got home, Uncle Kenneth told my parents that I'd been drinking, and all hell broke loose: my mother screaming and shouting the house down, my father with smoke coming out of his ears, ready to deliver a punishment that would make me a good girl for once and for all. Having said that, this was the umpteenth time all hell had broken loose in my house since I started at the Pres. I was always being sent up to Sister Columbia's office, mostly for disturbing the class in one way or another. Although in those years they didn't write letters home from school, word about my antics filtered home through the grapevine. Next thing, Daddy would be waiting for me, leather belt at the ready.

The rest of the year continued in much the same vein and into the summer. It's all a bit of a haze of acting out and getting punished at home, being cheeky to teachers and dossing off school. Much of my time at home was spent hidden under the blankets in bed, listening to Tony Prince of Luxembourg 208 on a transistor radio. That little radio and all the new music coming out of it had become my latest escape hatch.

In September, when I went back to school, there was great excitement about our first hop, which was to be held at the Bish on a Sunday afternoon. I had seen an all-in-one blue trouser suit in a magazine, and I wanted one just like it to wear to the hop. It had a zip down the front, was edged with white stitching, and had flaps on the tits, with pockets and more white stitching. Mammy and I came up with a pattern for it, and we made it together. Dressed in it, with my hair around my shoulders, I thought I was the most gorgeous thing ever to walk on two legs.

The hop was a crowd of awkward girls from the Pres and some even more awkward boys from the Bish, thrown together in a hall with bad music playing, Miwadi orange to drink, and nuns and brothers stiffly walking around all the time to make sure nothing immoral was going on.

We all tried to throw a few shapes, the girls dancing with the girls, the boys hanging around the edges of the hall, until the last song, Bob Dylan's 'I'll Be Your Baby Tonight' came on. Out of the crowd of Bish lads walked this black-haired boy, looking nervously but intently in my direction. 'Would you like to dance?' he asked, and next thing we were out on the floor, our hands on each other's waist, the prescribed twelve inches apart at all times, as the nuns and brothers policed the end of the slow set.

His name was Michael Connolly, and he had the most amazing brown eyes and a big, beautiful white smile that stretched across his whole face. I had never seen him before, even though he lived in Shantalla. He had been in boarding school up until his Inter Cert, and had just come home to go to the Bish.

I fell head-over-heels. There was something so gentle and soft about him, and he wasn't like other lads. He was a quietly thoughtful boy. And when it was all over, he walked me back to Ashe Road, holding my hand. I was on cloud-fucking-nine.

After that, Michael and I were constantly with each other. He would walk me to the Pres every morning, and after school we'd go walking out over the fields, picking blackberries. It was a really cold autumn that year, so we were always trying to keep warm. We would go into the Cathedral which had just been built in Galway, where there was underfloor heating.

One day, we were sitting on the floor in the nave, with its mosaics of John F. Kennedy and Pope Paul XXIII, when this man came in to hunt us out, demanding to know what we were doing, and saying he was going to tell our parents on us. 'Where are you from?' he snapped, and before I could get a word out of my mouth, Michael replied: 'Mayo.'

Eyeing us suspiciously, the man asked: 'Where in Mayo?'

'We're from Cong,' Michael replied, which must have been answer enough, because your man left us alone after that.

The most remarkable thing about the time Michael and I spent together was that we hardly ever talked to each other. Words didn't seem that important. I certainly never told him my father hit me. I would never have said it, because I was too ashamed.

After a couple of months wandering aimlessly around Galway, hand in hand, we decided we'd run away together. It seemed like the perfect solution. Things at home were going from bad to worse, and I was looking for more extreme escape routes.

We decided to steal a boat from the rowing club at UCG and sail up the Corrib to one of the islands, stocking up on Tayto and bars of Dairy Milk along the way. We had decided to be together for a night, so that we would know what it would be like to wake up in the morning with someone that you cared about. We wanted to go to sleep happy and to wake up happy, for once.

When we got to the island, we held hands in our customary way, talked and kissed and rolled around in the grass a bit, and generally froze, eking out our crisps and chocolate. It was the dead of winter by then. At least he was a warm kisser, and he had the most beautiful lips. There was no sex involved: it was very chaste, really. We were only a pair of starry-eyed kids.

At some stage, while we were sitting on the edge of the Corrib, shivering in the dark, I whispered: 'Say something nice to me, will ya?'

'Like what?' he asked, but I couldn't follow up on it. I wanted him to tell me that he loved me, because I genuinely and absolutely loved him. He couldn't say it, but I knew he felt the same as I did.

While we were freezing our arses off on that island of teen romance, half of Shantalla was out looking for us. I don't know who blew the whistle – maybe it was Kenneth, who was always looking out for my safety – but someone did anyway and, of course, everyone thought the worst.

Eventually we realised that it was far too cold to spend the night on the island, so we hopped into the boat and rowed back to Galway. All hell broke loose when we got home.

I didn't see or speak to Michael again for another forty years. He was sent away immediately, and I was put under lock and key. I nearly went demented, I was so distraught over losing him. Nobody would tell me where he was, and I couldn't find out. I couldn't for the life of me understand why they would want to break up something that was so loving and trusting and good.

Many years later, I was with talking Michael D. Higgins,

who said he had heard a story about a couple who had run away to the Island together and had written a poem based on it, called 'Corrib Love'. Later, when he sent me the poem, it made me cry.

When I went to my first therapist, after I stopped drinking in my thirties, she said: 'You should ring Michael up again.' She explained that the first love you ever have is probably the strongest and the most pure, because it comes without any personal agendas on either part.

When I started writing this book, I decided to take the bull by the horns and trace Michael through his sister, who still lives in Galway. He lives in York now, and fondly remembers as much of our relationship and island misadventure as I do, although he says that when we were on our long walks, I was constantly talking about my feelings, and trying to get him to do the same. So much for my memories of us hardly speaking!

With Michael gone, and me feeling like there was nothing to look forward to ever again, I started dossing from school and going with the girls to the Oyster Bar in Galway. I haven't grown an inch since I was thirteen, so I was tall enough for my age, with big tits already. Instead of a schoolbag, I carried a red cardboard folder with all my books in it, so that I looked like a student from UCG. We all did the same thing, to look like students.

We'd go into the Oyster Bar in the afternoon and drink vodka and lemonade. These were four pence each and I'd be locked after one. There used to be lads from the Bish in the pub as well. It was a dimly lit place with huge big sofa-type chairs, a low ceiling and cigarette smoke hanging in the air all the time. Sometimes we'd drink coffee, but if we were feeling particularly bold, we'd get pissed.

I got another boyfriend then, a gorgeous strapping lad called Michael Small. He was a couple of years older than me, and he would come to our house in the morning in his father's car, a Morris Oxford, to collect me and drive me to school. He'd be there waiting when I came out in the evening too, the car polished to a rich shine.

I was the envy of the school, of all the girls, and soon I began to have delusions of grandeur. I wanted to be like Michael Small. His sisters went to the Dominican College up on Taylor's Hill and his family had money. They had a big farm and they owned a butcher shop. Maybe this is why my mother liked him.

Mammy would tease me about him, singing 'The Butcher Boy', and I'd pretend to be annoyed, although I was secretly delighted. She asked me to bring him home to meet her one Sunday. She baked a big cake, had the tea out with cups and saucers and the whole shooting match, but he said he was in training for swimming, and would only take an apple and a glass of milk. She was well impressed by this.

Mostly we just sat in his car, talking about this and that, kissing every now and then. Deep down, I felt like a traitor to Michael Connolly. He was still there in my head all the time.

When Michael Small went back to boarding school in Limerick, he wrote me long letters, which I kept in a box for years, but it fizzled out fairly quickly. His best friend Johnny started hanging around with me. We were kind of commiserating about the fact that Michael wasn't around anymore, and one thing led to another. Johnny had it bad. A small, cute lad with a big head of brown curly hair, he was a really gentle character. A very creative soul. He would constantly write me poems and paint me pictures. There's still a picture that he painted for me in my father's house. Oddly enough, it is a painting of the island on the Corrib that Michael Connolly and I had run away to.

When I wasn't dossing from school, I was causing all sorts of disturbances in the classroom, which all seem to blend into one. By the time it was coming up to my Inter Cert, every teacher in the place hated me, and one day I must have done something that ended up being the straw that broke the camel's back. To this moment, I can't remember exactly what it was that I did – it's been conveniently shoved under the carpet in my own head. But it was bad enough for me to be hauled up to Columbia's office, and told in no uncertain terms to sling my hook. I was only allowed to come back to sit the exams.

Not that I gave a fuck about the Inter. I took the pain at home because of my school expulsion and sleepwalked through the exams, not really knowing what was coming next, and not really caring.

Over the summer, my mother went up to the Dominican College and begged them to take me in there. Now, this appealed to me greatly. Michael Small's sisters were both at the Dominican, and more than anything, I wanted to be like Michael Small's sisters. In a word, posh. So Mammy took me up to meet the headmistress, Sister Augustin – 'Gussie', as we called her – who said she would take me in, on one condition: that I promised to behave myself.

I promised faithfully. I said to myself: 'I'm going to be a real good girl up here and leave all that shit behind me.' And I really did think that I would turn over that new leaf. I started as I meant to go on, turning up in my neatly pressed uniform, ready to apply myself to the studies and be just like all the other girls at the Domincan. But every girl at the Dominican wasn't a good girl. There were some wild girls in the mix, and I gravitated towards them like a fly to shite.

The new gang was me, Catherine Geraghty and her sister, Margaret Geraghty – Big Gert and Little Gert – their family lived in Malawi, Africa, so they were boarding – Lorraine McDonagh, and Lorraine's sister, Celia. Lorraine and Celia had just come back to Ireland from Birmingham. Their father owned The Harbour Bar in Galway. The first day they walked into the school, they were completely dressed in black and they had naggins of vodka in their schoolbags. They were instantly in the club.

Of the whole crew, Catherine Geraghty, or Big Gert, stayed a lifelong friend. She was my bridesmaid at my second wedding – my mother wouldn't hear of her being my bridesmaid at my first – and during her speech at the meal, she remembered lots of the stuff we got up to, with me usually leading the brigade.

Like, for example, the time we blew up hundreds of balloons and pushed them out the windows of the Corrib restaurant, which was the highest building in Galway at the time. Or the time we all went to the Cathedral for confession, and one by one queued up to confess to the same poor unfortunate priest that we had been impregnated by the Holy Spirit and were about to deliver the virgin birth.

This was all at the beginning of fifth year, and the stuff we got up to was imaginatively bold, if you had to put a description on it. By the following summer, things would be entirely different. Instead of an odd vodka and lemonade at the Oyster Bar, I would be hanging around Eyre Square, off my head on acid: I had found an exciting, new and ultimately very dangerous way to escape the shameful secrets that were swimming just below the surface of my life.

5

'Listen to the Lion'

The first time I took LSD was on a beautiful summer's day in 1971. A bunch of the girls were with me, and we were hanging around with some much older lads. I remember a guy called JJ. He had long hair and sandals and was forever sitting cross-legged in Eyre Square, dispensing knowledge to the likes of us. We had all smoked a little bit of dope now and then in the music room at school, so taking acid didn't seem like a huge deal. I don't know exactly who handed over the tabs of 'yellow sunshine', but it was general knowledge that it was made by a student who was manufacturing the stuff in UCG. He and his girlfriend were handing it out free of charge. I didn't think twice about putting my half under my tongue.

By then, my reading had taken a giant leap, from Enid Blyton's *Malory Towers* to the likes of Jack Kerouac's *On the Road* and *The Prophet* by Kahlil Gibran, which was to become my bible. I knew that acid was big with hippies in America, and that it was supposed to be a life-changing experience, so I dived in with both eyes open. At fifteen years of age, on the farthest reaches of the west coast of Ireland, I thought I was supremely educated about the stuff.

We all took our half tabs and walked out to Salthill, waiting for something to happen. When we were out on the promenade, it kicked in. The feeling of going up was very gentle, and then suddenly, with the waves softly licking the strand and the sky as blue as a starling's egg, I entered what I could only describe then as 'a religious experience'.

I don't want to be singing the praises of Class A drugs, but at the time, acid kind of saved me – for a while anyway. It allowed me to see that life was bigger than me, that there were other ways of thinking, that change was possible. It opened me to a perspective beyond the narrow confines of the life I was living.

From an early age, I was a girl who longed for freedom, for independence and control of my own destiny, but my experience of the world had been the exact opposite of this. The more freedom I tried to take for myself, the more the people in my life tried to batten down the hatches and control me. Acid took me out of this contradiction. It allowed me freedom of thought, to explore other ways of living and thinking. Taking mind-altering drugs gave me secret self-control. For a while anyway.

Soon enough, free from my school uniform, I was the consummate weekend hippie. I made big long maxi-skirts and huge flared jeans, I wore headbands and flowers in my hair. We'd all drop acid and sit in the park tripping, or walk along Salthill with our heads in the sky. We'd lie in the grass in Eyre Square, watching the slow changes in cloud formations, every so often turning to smile at each other in our altered states. And when we were slowly coming down from our trips, we would talk about the meaning of life and find answers, real and true answers, although they didn't seem to make much sense the next day, until we got high again.

One evening we were sitting in Eyre Square when one of the lads, JJ maybe, came running up to us and said: 'Quick, quick, come and look! The hotel is full of ballet dancers.' We all trooped over to The Great Southern, where instead of ballet dancers, waiters were walking around. We had a good laugh, appreciating the hallucination, even if we weren't having it ourselves.

I began bringing acid with me everywhere. These days I wasn't carrying my schoolbooks in a red 'student's folder', but in a canvas army surplus bag with 'Ban the Bomb' logos drawn on it in black marker. I had a little troll doll with a shock of luminous green hair tied to the bag, and I kept my supply in its head.

At night in bed, I would take a little corner of a tab and trip away into the wee small hours, reading Aldous Huxley's *The Doors of Perception* or *The Teachings of Don Juan* by Carlos Castaneda. In the morning, I'd take some more and arrive in school high as a kite. Once we went to Limerick on a school day out to see Shakespeare's *King Lear*, and a few of us were tripping away on the bus. It was the most magical, if difficult-to-follow, production of a Shakespeare play I have ever seen. There wasn't a dry eye in the house, we were laughing so much – until Gloucester got his eyes gouged out, and I lost the plot. 'They're taking his eyes out! They're taking his eyes out!' I screamed, until eventually we were kicked out on our arses.

As time went on, we were all drinking anything we could lay our hands on when we were tripping, and when we weren't we would sit around smoking dope. We had a new girl in our gang called Mary too. I hung around with her all the time. She had an older boyfriend called Andy.

On Sundays, a few of us would go to this abandoned house in Salthill and hang around there, drinking Smithwicks or Harp from stolen barrels we pierced with screwdrivers before catching the beer that spouted out in a saucepan. After school, Mary and myself would head down to her house and listen to Jethro Tull and Rory Gallagher records. Mary was madly in love with Rory. Her mother was out at work all day, so we had the run of her place. Or we would go to the Oyster Bar. I remember a nun storming in there one day and booting us all out of the place.

One Saturday night we ended up at a party in a student house. It was there that I met Fintan Coughlan for the first time: the man I would end up marrying. But I also met Andy's older brother Felim, who was studying philosophy at UCG. There was an immediate attraction between us, although for all the wrong reasons.

Felim was the first person I met in my life who was as filled with teenage torment as I was.

We quickly became united in our angst. We started hanging out together all the time: talking and talking, drinking. I can't say we were having a laugh, because we were like a double act of misery and angst. We were helping each other carry the big heavy chips on our shoulders.

As much as Felim and I had issues with our parents, my

father had larger issues still with Felim. I thought it was because of the age gap between us, but it was probably more to do with the fact that I was running wild and Dad held Felim responsible. Whatever was the case, I was strictly forbidden to see him – which was like waving a red rag at a bull.

That Christmas, Felim gave me Van Morrison's *Saint Dominic's Preview*, although he wasn't allowed within fifty feet of the house at the time. It was Christmas Eve and I was in the sitting room listening to records when I heard this tapping on the window. There was Felim, standing outside in a jumper and a hat, his breath coming out in clouds of steam, bloody freezing to death. He handed me the wrapped-up album through the window and scurried off home before my father could catch him.

All through the Christmas holidays, I listened to Van Morrison singing 'Listen to the Lion' over and over again, and for the first time the words of a song began to speak to me, to echo my own experiences. The word 'soul' was mentioned in it a lot: 'I shall search my soul'. Before that, I had a vision of my soul being this kind of leather thing inside me that was stained with black marks of sin. I had no other concept of it. Connecting my soul to my emotional self was a completely new and beguiling idea to me.

Getting this album was a key moment in my journey towards becoming a singer: learning how lyrics can reach out beyond a song and grip a person, make them feel understood. The music of Van Morrison became very important to me, as did the songs of Leonard Cohen. However, I had no idea at the time how this music would go on to become central to my future. As ever, I was stuck in the present and I hadn't a clue what I was going to do beyond the next moment. The primary focus was on escaping.

Felim and I decided to run away. There was a house in Galway which was up for sale and empty. I packed up a few things and left home without a word of goodbye. We holed up in this house for a week, trying to figure out our next move. My abiding memory of being in that house is the cold and damp. We were fucking freezing. Felim's brother, Andy, brought us blankets from their house and a bit of food to keep us going, but it wasn't much.

We decided we would go to Dublin with the little bit of money we had between us and make a new life for ourselves there. So, one morning we woke up really early and walked up town to the station to get the 7.30 a.m. train out.

Of course, with me having disappeared for a week, my distraught parents had the authorities looking for us, and no sooner had Felim and I emerged into the cold light of day than we were apprehended by a member of the Garda Síochána. We were hauled into the police station, where both sets of parents came to get us, and that was that. We were forbidden to go near each other again, and this time I knew it was for real, that they would get their way and I wouldn't see Felim anymore. And I knew as well that I was going to get the worst beating of my life when I got home.

It's easy to look back on myself in those days and see a self-involved teenage nightmare who was causing grief for all her family. But in the thick of it, there was no seeing the wood for the trees. I was misunderstood; I was a victim; I was being forcibly separated yet again from a boy I thought I loved. I couldn't understand why my parents wanted to prevent me from being happy, yet it seemed like that is what they had made it their sole purpose in life to do.

When we got home, my father didn't beat me. He just sighed, gave me a look of utter disgust and went off into his beloved garage. My mother went into the sitting room and turned on the television.

I went upstairs, locked the bathroom door and tried to kill myself. I still have the scars on my arms from the damage I did. I took one of my father's old-fashioned razor blades and sat on the edge of the bath, hacking and hacking away at my wrists, waiting for something to happen: waiting to die. I was thinking: 'This is really going to fucking hurt them. This will make them pay.'

I wanted them to know how fucking miserable I was and what they had done to me. I imagined them kicking in the door, finding me dead, or maybe rescuing me, but nothing was happening. Downstairs I could hear canned laughter on the television.

Then, in the midst of all my tears and self-pity, blood start spouting out of my wrists and I began to get scared. It really bloody hurt. And I hadn't done it properly.

I opened the bathroom door, sat on the top stair and started screaming and screaming. The next thing my father was carrying me downstairs, my mother was crying and all my brothers and sisters were looking at me with wide, frightened eyes. I passed out before Daddy put me into the car to drive me to the hospital.

When I woke up in casualty at Galway Regional Hospital, with my wrists all stitched and bandaged up, the doctor stood over my bed and said: 'What you did was a criminal offence. Try it again and we'll call the guards.'

Now that's what I call bedside manner.

I was put on a ward upstairs. I remember a nurse saying to me: 'Look what you've done to your parents. How could you do such a thing?' Mammy and Daddy were sitting beside the bed, looking ten years older than the last time I had seen them.

The next day, a psychiatrist came to assess me and it was decided that I would be packed off to the nuthouse.

To this day, I can't pass the mental hospital in Ballinasloe without a shiver going down my spine. It is a huge, cold, grey, imposing building – like something out of a Dickens novel, if Dickens had been bog Irish.

When I walked, flanked on either side by my parents, through the massive, heavy front doors of the hospital, they were locked behind us. The minute we were inside, the smell of boiled cabbage and disinfectant hit my nose, and I could hear the sound of someone crying in the distance.

We were brought into an office, and while my parents spoke in whispers to the admitting doctor, I kept my head down, with my hair covering my face, saying not a word. I had decided I would have a philosophical approach to the place. I would observe it all and mentally note it down for my research on the human condition.

Before my parents left, I asked for cigarettes and my father went down the town to get me twenty Major. This was a massive gesture on his part, buying me fags. I'm sure his poor heart was broken, as was my Ma's. I remember her saying: 'Oh, Mary, what's happening to you? What's happening to you?' She was balling, crying her eyes out before they left.

I was put on a ward filled with old ladies who were in various states of mental health. The woman in the bed next to me was called Madelyn. She had long, neat grey hair, tied in a ponytail at her back, and she was always desperate for a cigarette, so desperate that she rolled up bits of old newspaper and smoked them. I tried that too.

There's no way to describe how time passes in a place like that. It inches along at a snail's pace, and every day and night is blended into one, and you don't feel time passing at all. I think I might have been sedated for much of the month I spent there.

There was nothing to do but wander around – no such thing as occupational therapy. You could either sit in the dayroom and look at the four walls, or you could walk the corridors, or you could sit on your bed and look at the four walls. I got on fine with some of the women on the ward, while I avoided others – the volatile ones –like the plague.

A desperate feeling of loneliness set in. I had some visitors: my uncle Kenneth, my parents. Big Gert came one day when my mother was there. Mammy told her to get out and not to tell anybody what I had done. A few years later, my mother wrote to Gert to apologise.

Whenever a visitor left, I would lie in my bed with the covers pulled over my head and think I was never going to get out of the place. I felt completely separated from the outside world, a million miles away from my friends and the things we used to get up to. But part of me didn't want to go back to that world. Under those covers or wandering those wards, there was a sense of safety too.

I was kind of excited about my first session with the psychiatrist. Having read R.D. Laing and Aldous Huxley, I was interested in the state of the mind and how we perceived the world around us. I talked to the psychiatrist about my experiences with LSD, but I didn't say what he wanted to hear. Instead I glorified acid, telling him how it was opening my mind, how it was my salvation.

Instead of exploring with me why a fifteen-year-old girl would think mind-altering drugs were her salvation, the good doctor just took copious notes in his little black book, and then reported to my parents that I was a drugs fiend.

My father's response was to beat it out of me. The day I was released from Ballinasloe, he took me into the front room and thumped me. He took all my maxi-skirts, my lovely flared jeans, my army surplus bag with its troll doll and threw them into the fire. This was what I got for disgracing him and the family, this was the last of my messing around with being a hippie and drugs. This was the end of it.

The whole affair was a disaster. But that's what happened to people at the time, I suppose. There were no social workers; there were no nice counsellors; there were no therapists. There were just fucked-up people trying to cope as best they knew how with things they had no understanding of.

Over the years, my father told me time and time again that he was beating me for my own good. His violence when I came out of the asylum was just more of the same. He really believed he was doing it for the right reasons, to make me good, to make me better, to stop me going down the road I'd started on when I was just a little girl.

I've long since come to accept my father's limitations, to forgive him and to love him. But at the time, I would not be broken by him, and my hatred for him coursed through my veins like venom.

I was very, very shaky in my first few days back at school after all this. I thought everyone was whispering about me, which they probably were. Attempted suicide and incarceration in a mental home are the stuff of a good gossip. On the face of it, I decided I would knuckle down and be good.

I felt that I had landed myself in an awful lot of trouble. I hadn't made any connection between the sexual abuse and the way I was behaving, and I wouldn't for a long time. But I knew I had to pull myself together and try to get on with things. Anything would be better than going back to Ballinasloe.

I began to look forward to English class. The teacher, Angeline Whelan was her name, imparted a great love for Shakespeare and John Donne, as well as all the poets: Keats, Shelley and Yeats. She was very nice to me, all the teachers were. Maybe they were being kind because of what happened, but somehow it didn't seem like that.

Once Angeline Whelan went sick, and she was replaced by a substitute English teacher called Pat Rabbitte, who would, of course, go on to be the leader of the Labour Party. The moment Pat walked into the class and introduced himself, I latched on to his surname and teased him incessantly, calling him 'Bugs Bunny' and all sorts of other stupid names. Eventually, he just exploded and dragged me up to 'Gussie's' office. 'Either she goes from the class or I go,' he told the headmistress. Guess which one of us left the class . . .

I remember this period as the happiest time in my secondary school life. There was a good bit of normality for a while. That year's school musical was *Goodnight Vienna*, and more than anything, I wanted to be in it. They gave me a small part in the chorus, and I was beside myself with delight. Some of the girls played soldiers, but I was one of the women in the chorus and had this great big dress to swish around in. My parents came to the show and they were proud of me, and for a brief minute it was a bit like Enid Blyton, like I had ended up in Malory Towers at last.

But as time went on, it was back to the same old story with the girls: off down the town, smoking dope, drinking. I was mad for excitement, for demented stuff, and there was just no stopping myself. I was determined to have a good time, and this was the way I thought I could have it.

I continued doing whatever the hell I wanted to do, and taking the consequences. I was mad to go to this music festival on the Aran Islands with Planxty and Christy Moore and Donovan playing, but my parents were having absolutely none of it. On that Saturday morning, instead of going to work at the GTM, I went down to the quays and got a boat to Inis Mór. I'd left a note on my bed, saying: 'Mam and Dad, I'm gone to Aran with the girls. See you all on Sunday night.'

On the boat on the way over, I met this guy called Martin Egan: his nickname was 'Irish'. Martin taught me to sing the song 'Peggy Gordon'.

I would come across him busking on Grafton Street in Dublin many years later. When I leaned over to give him some money, he said: 'You don't know me, do you?'

I was looking at him like he had ten heads. He said: 'I'm "Irish",' and he sang 'Peggy Gordon' for me. He's actually done well for himself in the meantime, writing a few songs for Christie Moore.

When I got home from Aran, my father was waiting outside the gate for me, strap in hand.

Writing this memoir, I realise that I have painted a certain picture of my father during those years, an unremittingly dark picture. But there were moments of light and a shared sense of humour between us. I didn't lick it off the trees, as they say.

Once, when I was pretending to do my homework but was listening to Leonard Cohen singing 'Suzanne' on our little red and white record player instead, my father poked his head around the door and said: 'Do you know where that fucker lives?'

I said: 'Canada, or America, or somewhere like that,' to which he replied: 'If you ever get his address, I'll send him a packet of Anadin to put him out of his misery.'

I think Daddy recognised that I was in pain, but he was at a complete loss about what to do with me at the same time. To him, I was just this out-of-control wild child. In many ways he was right.

I wanted to have sex, to lose my virginity, but none of the guys I ever dated would do it with me. They kept telling me they had too much respect for me, which I couldn't understand. If they respected me, why couldn't they give me what I wanted?

Luckily the Lord was at hand, or more like some self-appointed messengers of the Lord. The summer before my Leaving Cert year, a big, multi-coloured double-decker bus rolled into town and parked itself in Eyre Square. It disengorged a group of very clean-cut, outrageously good-looking hippies – mostly American – called the Children of God. They were on a mission to get the legions of Galway to join their cult. I started hovering around that bus like a bee around a honeypot.

I hadn't the slightest bit of interest in the Christianity they were selling, but I did have my eye on one particular member of their pack. Tony was his name and he looked like the Jesus in the picture of the Sacred Heart that hung in my mother's kitchen. His glossy hair was long and dark and his brown eyes looked at you from underneath their lids, in the same way Princess Diana would look at Prince Charles a few years later.

The first time Tony and I met, he brought me on board the magical bus and chatted me up with bits of scripture. I pretended to be very interested in the Bible passages he was quoting, but really I was imagining kissing him and running my hands through his gorgeous hair. The second day, we took a stroll out to Salthill, where he chatted to me more about the Children of God. They believed that God created human sexuality, that it is a natural, emotional and physical need, and that as such sex is a pure and natural wonder of God's creation. Which was all fine by me.

Tony kissed me and we ended up having it off on the rocks

at the far end of Salthill beach, the waves rolling in limply on the sand, as I discovered what all the talk was about. In keeping with most first sexual experiences, it was vaguely uncomfortable and over very quickly. Suffice to say, there were no fireworks involved.

The Children of God bus moved on from Galway the next day and I never saw Tony again, but I was hardly devastated. I didn't tell the girls about the encounter. I didn't want anyone to think I was a slut. Looking back on it, I was far too young to do what I did, but then again, sex has been messed-up in my mind from a very early age. As young as I was, after Tony I felt more grown-up than ever.

My final year at school played out much in the fashion I had become used to, with me getting up to the usual stuff. My teachers had pretty much given up on me. Me and Angela became friendly with some people from the Bahá'i community in Galway, who would often be on Shop Street selling bracelets and pendants made from horseshoe nails.

We loved the way these people were about one world, one religion. Their founder, a Persian called Bahá'u'lláh, was stoned to death for his beliefs in the 1860s. He believed that all people were equal, both men and women. That wasn't very popular in his day.

They had some great ideas, the Bahá'i, and they were lovely people. Some of them became lifelong friends. Our father thought they were from the devil, of course, and tried everything in his power to stop us from going near them. These people were so clean-living, it wasn't even funny. They didn't drink, they didn't smoke, they didn't believe in sex before marriage. If Daddy had had a lick of sense, he would have been encouraging me to join up.

I knew I wasn't going to go to college. My sole plan was to get away from my family, and I was biding my time. I was really sad that I wouldn't be going to college, because I had a thing for learning, but I felt I had no choice. If I had gone, it would have been in Galway, because that would have been the only way for us to afford it. But I knew I had to leave home. I had to get out.

A few months before my Leaving Cert, my youngest sister, Carol, started to get a sore back. It turned out to be a rare disease of the spine, and she was hospitalised for nine months.

Poor Carol was a really sporty type. Both she and my brother Gerard were mad into the Community Games and winning medals for running and jumping. But this effectively put an end to all that. Carol's surgery involved taking pieces of her hip and putting them into her spine. She was lying in a full-body plaster cast for nine months.

I remember going to see Carol in hospital, knowing that I probably wouldn't be seeing her for much longer, because it was in my head to go away. I didn't have a care in the world about leaving and I didn't give a fuck whether I got the Leaving Cert or not, because I wouldn't be around to be ashamed if I failed miserably.

A few days after the exams finished, I quietly packed my bags and left a note on my bed. It was that famous quote from *The Prophet* by Kahlil Gibran: 'Your children are not your children. They are the sons and daughters of Life's longing for itself. They come through you but not from you. And though they are with you, yet they belong not to you.'

I didn't cry and I didn't hesitate on the doorstep. I ran all the way down Ashe Road with my little bag, past Dooley's shop, past the clinic, past the hospital and I was free. Free of my parents at last, free of the house next door and the betrayal of my uncle. Free as a bird.

6

'Tambourine Man'

Leaving home coincided with the first time I ever sang in public as an adult. Myself and the two Gerts – Catherine and Margaret – hitched to Ennistymon in County Clare, where there was a trad festival going on, and we hung around there for my first week of freedom. We hadn't a red cent between us, so we were living from hand-to-mouth with whatever we could get. Ennistymon is a beautiful, picturesque little town, and it was packed that week with people enjoying the summer sunshine. There were buskers on every corner, plying their trade. We decided to pitch in our lot with them, and soon we were making money for cider as I sang the few traditional songs I knew and the Gerts collected the cash in their hats.

One day we were spending our hard-earned busking money in a pub where there were all these traditional Irish musicians having a great old session: fiddle players, mandolin players, guitarists, a guy on the accordion, a few bodhráns. There was great singing going on. Various individuals who were just in to have a pint and listen to the music would burst into song now and then. I knew the words of 'Peggy Gordon', which Martin Egan had taught me on the boat to Aran, so I took my turn and belted it out.

People were kind of taken with it. I got a good round of applause and calls for more, so I sang an English song made famous by Gay Woods called 'The Blacksmith'. I enjoyed the feeling I got from singing for people, in tune with the instruments, and I was surprised by my own voice, but beyond that I didn't think anything of it. It was just a singsong in a pub, and the landlady gave us free drinks and our dinner – a big plate of bacon and cabbage – for it.

I got talking to the guy playing the accordion, a soft-spoken man called Robert. He told me he was there with a crowd of people who lived as part of a commune, camping in Gort, County Galway. After the session, me and the girls went back to his van with him and met some of the group, including a couple called Robin and Linus and their children.

I was fascinated with them all. They were major, big-time hippies: the men with long hair, straggly beards and beads around their necks, the women in long, flowing dresses, smelling of patchouli oil. It was 1973, the year flower power finally reached the shores of Ireland, and I was delighted to be suddenly in the thick of it.

They were a nice bunch of people, relaxed and friendly, and I quizzed them until the wee small hours about their lives in the camp in Gort. By the time the sun came up, I had made the decision to join them.

The fact that I fancied the arse off Robert might have had some part in my coming to that conclusion. He was an

American hippie, like the real ones who had been at Woodstock. He had a big head of strawberry blond curls and twinkly blue eyes, framed by little John Lennon glasses. Everything about him said 'sophisticated hippie' to me, from the red neckerchief tied at an angle around his neck, to his faded denim dungarees, hand-knit socks and sandals. There was a self-confidence about him that was very alluring – you didn't see it much in Irish men.

As the Fleadh came to a close, the Gerts went back to Galway, wishing me luck on my travels, and I went to Gort to begin my life as a fully-fledged hippie. Robin and Linus lived in a house on the estate at Lough Cutra Drive, where coincidentally my grandmother and mother came from. The house acted as a kind of centre for everyone to gather in, surrounded by lots of caravans.

Robert and I shared his green canvas-topped gypsy caravan, kitted out with everything we needed inside. It was like a little treasure trove in there, full of nooks and crannies to hide things, the wooden shelves and walls painted in beautiful, traditional gypsy patterns. A little black stove in the corner kept us warm at night, and was somewhere to boil the kettle for a cup of tea.

Outside, a couple of goats were tethered to trees with rope, a few chickens roamed about the place, and some dogs. There were more horses than I could count, or maybe it was just that they all just looked like each other, so I could never tell exactly how many there were.

There was a constant smell of charred wood and smoke from the open fire, which everyone would sit around, smoking dope. This was the main activity of the place, along with going into Gort to the pub for pints on dole day. Robin and Linus turned out to be a pair of British society dropouts who had bought the house and set up this new world for themselves.

For the first few weeks, I felt in I was in complete Utopia. Out from under my father's control and away from the sins of the past, this easy-come, easy-go world, where people accepted me at face value and never seemed to place any judgement on anyone, made me feel like I had died and gone to heaven. You could have painted yourself bright green and hung naked from the tops of the trees in that place, and nobody would have batted an eyelid. I was having a great time with Robert in our little caravan, and getting on well with everyone in the group, but soon the hippie sheen began to fade.

Within a week of my arrival, the realities behind the apparent idyll of hippiedom began to hit home. With no hot running water, the resulting personal hygiene issues made the place far less attractive than I had previously imagined. The rose-tinted spectacles began to come off.

One day, Robert was going to Gort town in the van to do a bit of wheeling and dealing with horses and I went with him. While he was about his business, I snuck into a hotel, up the stairs and into one of bathrooms that were along the corridors. I locked the door and had a long, hot bath, washing the filth out of my hair, with the water turning brown from the muck from my feet and under my nails.

After a while I couldn't hack it anymore. The hippie life, which I had thought was as glamorous and sunshine-filled as Woodstock, was actually quite boring, damp and unhygienic. I told Robert that I was leaving. He shrugged his shoulders, gave me a kiss and a lift into Gort, so I could get on the main Galway to Limerick road and start hitching.

From the friendships I had made with the Bahá'i in Galway, I had a few tenuous connections in Limerick. Few people had telephones in those days, but I knew of a guy called Gerry who had a pub on Denmark Street, so I went there. Gerry directed me to Diane, a mother of one of the Bahá'i women in Galway, and her partner, Mick. They knew an Australian guy who lived in a big house on Patrick Street and he had rooms to let. You shared a kitchen with all the other people in the house and you had your own bedroom.

To pay the rent, I went out looking for a job, and ended up waitressing at a place called the Galleon Grill. I was delighted with myself. This at last was the independent life I had craved. I was earning money, I was away from home and I had my own place. It was a tiny attic room under the eaves, with a single bed in the corner and a rickety old chest of drawers shoved up against one wall. I painted the wooden floor apple green, bought a bunch of daffodils and put them on the windowsill, and burned a little incense. Lying on my bed there after an evening's work, I was happier than I had ever been. I was absolutely on my own, but I wasn't in the slightest bit lonely. I hadn't contacted my family in three months and I had no intention of getting in touch. They had other ideas, though.

Through the Bahá'i in Galway, Mammy and Daddy found out where I was working and one day, out of the blue, they turned up in the Galleon Grill. The minute I saw them, my heart sank. I was full sure they were there to take me home, no matter what I wanted for myself, and I resolved that my father would have to knock me out and shove me into the boot of the car if he wanted to get me back to fucking Shantalla.

I remember being out on the street, telling them how happy I was, that they needn't worry about me one little bit. I took them to see my lovely apple green room, but Dad's face fell. Really that house on Patrick Street was nothing but a tenement, but to me at the time it was a palace. I thought everyone would see it that way.

Daddy pleaded and begged me to come back home, but I think Mammy was there to satisfy herself that I had a job and a place to live, that I was doing okay for myself. In the end they went back home to Galway without me, and I surprised myself by feeling a bit tearful as their little car drove off down Patrick Street.

Working at the Galleon Grill, I had discovered a great love for chatting my head off with the customers, and I was making great tips. One night, not long after my parents' visit, about six really exotic-looking types came in for a meal. I was fascinated by them and, through hovering around their table, picking up what I could of their conversation, I discovered that they were from the Limerick College of Art. They were talking about how it was a pity that there were no live models for the students to draw.

I sat down with them and volunteered my services. The way I figured it, I could make some extra money during the day and keep my Galleon Grill job going at the same time.

To my dying day, I will never forget my first day as an artist's model. I knew that I would have to take all my clothes off, but I didn't realise how nerve-racking it was going to be. I was of the mindset that I could do anything, because I was free to do whatever I liked.

The students were all huddling over their easels, looking at me like a crowd of rabbits caught in headlights, even more scared than I was. This was the first time a model had ever posed naked in the college.

I was literally shaking from head to toe when I slipped my dressing gown off. I lay down on a foam mattress, surrounded by electric bar heaters, and tried to cover my bits and pieces with my hair, which was waist length at that stage. For the first ten minutes, I'm sure my entire body was puce, I was so embarrassed. Then I began to get bored. Life modelling is basically just hours and hours of sitting, lying, standing, doing this, doing that, trying not to move a muscle for maybe thirty minutes at a time. Still, it paid well, fifty pence an hour, as I recall, so I lasted for a good while. Doreen, the wife of one of the lecturers, still sends me a bunch of flowers every time I perform in Limerick.

My modelling job at the college elevated me into another echelon of hippiedom. It was the 1970s in Ireland, and for some reason, the whole Californian ethos of sunshine and free love had hit Limerick with a big bang. One of the people who had been chatting in the Galleon Grill that evening was the artist and head of the Art College, Dietrich Blodau, who lived in Rathkeale Manor in Adare. This was a massive, opulent house, full of sweeping staircases and man-sized open fireplaces with practically whole trees burning in them. There,

Dietrich hosted wonderful parties: those lucky enough to get an invitation would never forget the experience. These parties were wild and packed with people who were the opposite of everything I had grown up to expect from Irish people. Catholic repression didn't have a look-in here. All sorts of nationalities were at these parties. I remember an American girl called Colleen Kelly playing the guitar and singing Jefferson Airplane songs by a big, open fire, her long, straight, blonde hair just like Joni Mitchell's.

One party weekend, I stayed at the manor and ended up talking with an artist, who said he wanted to paint me. In the middle of the night, he came to my bedroom and lifted me out of the big iron bed, completely naked. He brought me to the bathroom and laid me down in the bath, saying: 'I want to paint you here.'

I was a bit cold – central heating was unheard of in that big house – but I didn't want to interrupt the creative flow of this great artist who wanted to immortalise my seventeen-year-old self, so I said nothing and let him get down to work. After a while he paused, looked up and said: 'Now, can we have sex?'

So we went back to my bed and did the deed, only in the middle of it, I got absolutely grossed out and told him to stop. I'd say he was a good fifteen years older than me. He didn't want to stop, so I pulled away and said: 'Fuck off out of my room and leave me alone.'

It was a bit of a turning point. I realised that the 'free love' ethos of the hippie life was definitely not for me.

The next morning, I went downstairs and Dietrich's mother-in-law brought me out to the greenhouses, where she grew millions of red and green peppers. It was the first time I had ever seen a pepper in my life. 'What the fuck do you do with those things?' I was thinking. Mrs Blodau brought some back to the kitchen to cook up for breakfast.

Felim Burke and I kind of rekindled our relationship around this time, and he came to visit me on a couple of occasions, but it wasn't anything as heavy as the relationship we had back in Galway. He persuaded me to come home for a big party one weekend in October. I knew the Gerts would be there, and I was dying to see them, having been separated from my friends for so long.

The decision to go to that party turned out to be a life-changing one, because it was there that I met Fintan Coughlan for the second time.

Fintan had just finished a philosophy degree at UCG and had come back to Galway after spending the summer in London. He had masses of long, flowing black hair and a matching beard, and kind, intelligent eyes, and was very well read and articulate. Right from the moment we started talking, there was a strong intellectual connection between us.

The party was a pretty wild affair, and many of Fintan's friends, who would become friends in my life in the years to come, were there, including Liam Gavin and Marty Hehir, Frank Kelly and Nhoj, which was John spelled backwards. Nhoj was the most exotic creature on earth, mad into Nietzsche. They were a very philosophical bunch of guys, all crazy about Wittgenstein, who had once taken up residence in Clifden. With all sorts of mad carry-on happening around us at that party, Fintan and I chatted and chatted about everything but the kitchen sink, discovering more and more in common with each other as the night went on.

I remember being a little awestruck by him. He was unlike any man I had ever talked to. He knew a huge amount about art and literature and politics, and expressed himself with eloquence and a sense of humour. He had a leadership quality about him: he made me think, he made me laugh, and I found myself hanging on his every word.

Fintan and I got together that night and became an item immediately. He visited me in Limerick the next week, and kept coming back after that. As time went on, I started feeling emotions I hadn't experienced since I ran away to that Corrib island with Michael Connolly.

There was a deep well of unhappiness in Fintan too, something that echoed the unspoken sadness in me. When Fintan and his brother Liam were very young, their mother had had a massive stroke. The boys were sent away to boarding school at St Mary's College in Galway.

When their mother was hospitalised for the long term in Merlin Park, Galway, their father moved down so he could be near her. By the time I met him, Fintan was settled in the city too.

He wasn't the first person I slept with, but Fintan was the first person I ever had a grown-up relationship with. We were equals, learning from each other and, I suppose, going together into the adventure that was adulthood. He was twenty and I was seventeen.

While in Limerick, I had stayed in contact with a guy called Mick Fraser, who hung around with the Bahá'i in Galway. Mick wrote to me about the squatting scene in London, where loads of Irish were living in abandoned houses, seemingly living the life of Reilly. So Fintan and I decided to head over there.

We made a plan. We would work in London for the winter, squatting so we didn't have to pay rent, and when we had saved enough, we would take off and travel the world together.

Before we went to London, I decided that I had to come to some conclusion about what had happened with my grandfather and uncle during my childhood in Galway. I hadn't ever spoken to anyone about it, but the more intimate I became with Fintan, the more it was on my mind.

I decided that I would tell my mother what happened. So one Saturday, I went to the house in Shantalla. I asked Mammy if I could speak to her in the sitting room, which raised an eyebrow immediately. The sitting room was the 'good room', a place used only at Christmas and when visitors were in the house.

Mustering up as much courage as I could, I tried to find the words to explain to Mammy what happened to me with my grandfather. I remember her silently sitting on the edge of the couch, her eyes growing wider and wider, as I recounted what had happened.

When I was finished, she screamed: 'That's a lie! You are never, ever to speak to your father about this, do you hear me? Never.'

'It's fucking true!' I screamed back at her. 'I'm not lying, I swear!' And that was it. She got up and left the room, and it wasn't spoken of again.

I was stunned and angry, but deep inside, a little voice was telling me: 'She's right, you weren't really abused. You let them do it. You didn't stop them and you didn't say a word. So *you* were responsible for whatever happened. If it was anyone's fault, it was your own.'

Fintan and I were on the next boat out to London, and I waved good riddance to Galway, to Ireland and to my past. As far as I was concerned, if the place was sinking to the bottom of the sea, I wouldn't throw it a lifering.

Together with Mick Fraser, we moved into a squat at 17 Endsleigh Road in West Ealing. There were six or seven terraced houses on the street, all occupied by a raggle-taggle bunch of hippies and dropouts. The people who had established the squat knew how to do everything. They had rigged the meters and pipes so you could get gas and electricity completely gratis.

Fintan and me settled into our room, with its mattress on the floor and its electric bar heater, and made it a cosy little space of our own with candles and incense and throws. We were both into Bob Dylan. Fintan had a guitar, which he played all the time. He taught me how to play 'Tambourine Man' and Leonard Cohen's 'Suzanne' and Neil Young's 'Harvest' in our little hideaway. Mostly Fintan would play and I would sing, and we were as happy as the day was long.

Every Saturday, we would go down to the Electric Cinema in Portobello together and watch a film. We loved the same movies, the same directors, the same actors. We had a lot in common and I felt we were on a mind-expanding trip together.

There was an American guy called Alan living in the house with us and, God love him, he was one of the worst junkies I've ever come across. All he did was take acid. I don't think he ever slept. Instead, he spent his time painting the walls and floor of his bedroom with tiny, intricate little spirals, triangles and squiggles. That's what he did, all day, every day.

When Alan couldn't get acid, he sniffed glue. I came home one night and he was in the sitting room with his head in a big plastic bag of Evo-Stik. He looked up at me and his face was all black, his beard covered in bits of stinking glue. I didn't know what the fuck he was doing, and laughed out loud at the sight of him. I was still a bit naïve in some ways. Poor Alan died in India a few years later.

There were only ever a couple of people in the squat earning money at one time, so we used to cook dinner in a big pot on the electric cooker in the kitchen and share it out: lentil stews and chilli con carne, which I had never heard of before, and chicken curries. There were some very lean times, when we'd all be putting as many vegetables as we could get into the pot, and padding the meal out with loads of rice.

In the evenings after dinner, we sat around and talked to each other. Those nights were like humongous group therapy sessions. Later, the guitars and Alan's bongo drums would come out and the singing would start. I only sang as part of the group, humming along with the choruses. I had become shy about my voice and would only sing a whole song by myself upstairs, cloistered away with my man.

Christmas came and a few people went home for the holidays. Fintan and I stayed on, but both of us were absolutely skint and starving. Luckily a package arrived from Mammy containing boxes of my favourite food at the time: Vesta beef and chicken curries, which were dry powdered concoctions that you mixed with water and heated up until the bits of reconstituted chicken or beef expanded. Granny included a box of USA biscuits in the package, which went down very well, and we had a grand Christmas, just the pair of us.

In January, two things happened: I got a job, and I discovered I was pregnant. The job was in a health food shop and café at Ealing Broadway tube station. My pregnancy, however, wasn't the healthiest, since I was doing plenty of acid and smoking dope, day in, day out, from the time I conceived to the time I took the test. I don't think Fintan was too enamoured of the fact that we were with child, but I was absolutely thrilled. Really scared, but delighted too. This baby was going to have the best life any child ever had. I would love it and teach it and bring it up safe and happy.

I told everyone in the squat my great news. The poor eejit that I was: it makes my heart sore to look back on it.

Through my work in the health food shop, Fintan and I discovered a thing called macrobiotics. It's a whole way of life, based on the belief that the food you eat powerfully affects your health and happiness. You steer clear of processed foods, and eat mostly wholegrain cereals, pulses, vegetables, seaweed, brown rice and fruit. Different dishes are cooked according to what time of year it is, and you balance the 'yin' and 'yang' of different ingredients in each dish, depending on what way you want your diet to affect your well-being. Yin foods are stimulating foods, while yang foods are relaxing, and your meals should never have too much of one or the other.

We became so serious about it all that we went to a talk by Michio Kushi, who was the Japanese father of macrobiotics.

During the talk, we sat there, completely in awe of him. I even went to a cookery class with his wife, Aveline.

My favourite dish at this time was a thing called a *hiziki* roll. *Hiziki* was a kind of seaweed. I would cook the stuff up with onions, then make a pastry with barley flour and water, roll the seaweed up in it and bake it. To the uninitiated, it might sound hard to believe, but it was absolutely gorgeous.

The one record I had brought from Ireland with me was by the folk band, Tir na nÓg: their first album, which I loved. So, you can imagine the excitement one day when the band's members, Sonny Condell and Leo O'Kelly, walked into the health food café. I nearly fucking wet myself! I asked them for their autographs and they happily obliged, enquiring about where I was from and how I was enjoying London. I was utterly star-struck and almost speechless.

One night, Fintan and I had a roaring, screaming row: our first. I don't have a clue what it was all about, probably something ridiculously stupid, considering the pattern of rows that would subsequently develop, but I do remember that in the course of that row, we did vindictive things to each other. Fintan melted my Tir na nÓg album over the electric fire, and I smashed his guitar in two over the back of a chair. Eventually we kissed and made up and vowed never to fight like that again.

In the early spring, Fintan got a job as a gardener with Acton Council, and one morning when he had gone to work, I woke up to find blood on the sheets. I went downstairs and found the only other person in the house, a guy from Limerick called Paul. He brought me to Middlesex Hospital, where I was told that I had miscarried. I remember the nurses being very concerned that I was seventeen and had been pregnant.

When it was all over and I was back at home with Fintan, I felt a flood of relief. Back in the real world, I saw what a terrible situation it would have been, to bring a baby into the squat.

On my eighteenth birthday, we went to see Rod Stewart in Watford. For the occasion, I made a skirt and embroidered the bottom of it. I felt that I was a fully grown-up woman. The summer was coming and with it, my friends, the two Gerts and Lorraine and Celia McDonagh, would be arriving in London. Fintan's mates, Marty Hehir and Liam Gavin, were already living down the road from us.

Fintan heard that Acton Council was looking for street sweepers and the money was better than what I was earning at the health food shop, so I applied for the job and got it. When the girls came over, three of them – the two Gerts and Lorraine – got jobs with me and soon we found ourselves on the same beat together, the first ever female street sweepers in the boroughs of Acton and Ealing.

It was a glorious summer. We wore dungarees and had a big push-along bin, which we'd roll along the road and put our sweepings into, and we were a very efficient team indeed, to begin with. It turned out we were cleaning the roads too quickly, and it was knocking the other street sweepers' noses out of joint. If the Gaffer, Old Ray, saw how fast we were, the other sweepers would have to work that quickly too, and they had a system going which made life much less stressful. They told us to slow down or else.

We would start the day at six in the morning, sweep for a

little bit and then go to a local caf for breakfast. While we were in the caf, the men would hide our brushes and we were supposed to just get lost for a couple of hours and come back for lunch. After lunch, we'd get our brushes back, and we could sweep for a few hours until Old Ray came around.

As long he saw us sweeping, our timesheet could be signed and then we would be free for the rest of the day. After knocking off, we would buy really cheap pink sparkling wine or cider, sunbathe and drink ourselves into the giggles in Acton Park.

During that summer, Fintan got a bit interested in Scientology, and the whole Dianetics side of it. This was the idea that tapping into the unconscious mind could cure all sorts of illnesses and unwanted emotions. It was believed that when people were in the womb, sleeping, unconscious in surgery, or otherwise knocked out, their minds were still receiving information. Whatever happened to them at these times stayed with them forever, and could lead to the disturbances that caused illnesses. Marty and Liam were into the concept too and I remember long conversations between the three of them about how Dianetics was the way forward with medicine and psychiatry. They all got fed up of it quickly enough.

Not being the scientific type, I became involved for a time with a crowd of Druids instead. I went to a few meetings about harnessing the magical power of the natural world, and liked what I heard. We then all went off to Stonehenge for the summer solstice. This was before Stonehenge was closed down to the public, in 1985. In those days, it was an intimate gathering of people who celebrated the longest day of the year and the death and regeneration of nature, partying until the dawn of the next day – there were nothing like the thousands of people who turn up these days, now that Stonehenge is open again.

Summer turned to autumn and, as the Gerts' thoughts turned towards going back to Galway to start college, mine and Fintan's returned to our travel plans. Lorraine and Celia were staying in London; Marty and Liam were moving to Paris.

Fintan and I had decided to go to Amsterdam and get the Magic Bus from there all the way to Athens, and then ferry out to the Greek islands, where all the hippies were going at the time. We were saving like mad for the trip, and were very excited at the prospect of it all. After Greece, we thought we might go to India. The world was our oyster.

Out of the blue, a letter from Fintan's father arrived. His mother's condition had taken a turn for the worse and she only had a little time left on this earth, so the prodigal son had to return. With our plans to travel to Greece put on hold, I decided to go back to Galway with Fintan.

Although I was disappointed, I felt things would be okay as long as we were together. We loved each other and we were only going home for a short while. We would be able to travel once Fintan had seen out his responsibilities. Little did I know that we were on our way back to square one, that the move would be permanent and that the disappointment Fintan felt about not being able to go on his big adventure would seep into our relationship, until all that was left of it was me, less than a decade on, by myself at the age of twenty-seven, and with three children.

7

'Daisy Lady'

When I arrived home, Fintan had already moved back into his father's house, but no fucking way was I going back to Shantalla. I met a guy called Patsy McGarry, who is now the religious affairs correspondent for *The Irish Times*, who lived with some friends in a house in Salthill. They were looking for somebody to live in the garage part, which had been converted into a bedsit. So I went to live there.

To pay the rent, I got a job minding the children of two doctors in the Regional Hospital. Their children were beautiful, happy-go-lucky little things with jet black hair. I looked after them in the mornings.

In the evenings, our social life resumed. Galway was, and still is, a very sociable town. There's an ease of meeting people about the place that's rare. You can be walking down the street, come across a stranger out of the blue, and soon you'll be firm friends. You can walk into one of the pubs any day, and bump into an old buddy, or meet someone new. I think, as a town, it is unique on the planet in this way – and I have been in many towns and cities.

One day, I saw this tall, skinny, bearded guy in town, walking down Shop Street, carrying a sack on his back and pushing a bicycle. I was strangely attracted to him and wanted to find out what he was about, so in that Galway way, I stopped to have a chat. We found ourselves standing there, shooting the breeze for the next half an hour, until his wife came along.

Both American, their names were John and Cindy Dring. John was a clinical psychologist, working as a research assistant at UCG. Cindy was a care worker with Holy Family School in Galway, which educated and cared for children with disabilities. Within the week, myself and Fintan were firm friends with John and Cindy. They would become a great influence on me.

We were all out having a few pints in a bar in Salthill called The Cottage one evening, and there were two musicians playing in the corner. I was really struck by both of them and the way they were playing their twelve-string guitars. It was a classical sound, and totally unlike anything I had ever heard pub session musicians playing before.

When they had finished playing, I got talking to them. One of them was called Erik and the other Michelle: they were Dutch and French respectively. They were looking for a place to stay, so I said: 'There's a room at our house. It's just down the road.'

And that's where my friendship with Erik Visser began. Of course I couldn't know then that Erik would become a key figure in my career in the music business, since at the time, I didn't have the slightest ambition to have a career, never mind the inkling of an idea that I could actually sing for a living.

Over the next couple of weeks, I missed my period, and even before I got the test, I knew I was pregnant again. This time I wasn't so delighted. The winter had set in and I was freezing in my garage bedsit. My glory days of freedom were down the toilet and I would sit, bundled up in the blankets on my bed, wondering how I could have been such a stupid fucking bitch to get pregnant again.

I knew nothing about sex, or, more importantly, contraception. We were a generation who were freely having it off with each other, but not one of us had been educated about birth control. This was long before the pill became available to people in Ireland. I had never even heard of a condom.

Fintan was deeply unhappy. His mother was dying, he was living at home with his father and his girlfriend was pregnant again. We hadn't travelled the world, we'd only got as far as London. Like me, Fintan didn't want to be back in Galway. We both felt trapped. After a summer exploring exciting, new alternative ways of living, we were going to have to settle down and become straight people.

We began fighting a lot. We would have these passionate screaming matches, throwing things, breaking stuff, clattering each other: nasty, vicious rows.

You would think, given our feelings and fights, that we would have steered well clear of the option of getting married, but for one reason or another, we didn't. To be a teenage girl and pregnant in Ireland at the time was to be a kind of pariah – the Magdalen Laundries were still thriving. Even though we hung out with a crowd of people who wouldn't have given a flying fuck whether we were married or not, Fintan and I came from traditional Catholic families, and, whether we admitted it to our hippie selves or not, our families had a major influence on us.

My mother was all for the marriage, although my father, in his typical way, didn't have much time for Fintan. As it stood, Fintan's father would not let me beyond the front door of his house, which was consecrated to the Blessed Virgin. He was a fervently religious man, and I think as far as he was concerned, I was some Shantalla slapper, pregnant with his son's illegitimate child. Fintan and I had many fights about it, me going on and on at him about how he wouldn't fucking stand up to his father and bring me into the house, and Fintan in the middle of it all, trying to please everyone.

We decided the only way around it was to get married, which was completely against our principles. The wedding was organised: I would walk up the aisle when I was three months pregnant, so I wouldn't be showing too much.

In the days and weeks that led up to the wedding, I became closer and closer to Erik. I was becoming more and more fascinated with the way he made music, how he worked at it. He practiced and practiced every day, he didn't just go down to the pub and play for the craic. And the sounds he could create! I would spend hours listening, really listening, to him play. The woman downstairs would complain because he tapped his foot on the bare floorboards as he played, so he would put a cushion under his foot to muffle the sound.

Looking back on it, there was a *ménage à trois* of sorts

between myself, Fintan and Erik. There was no sex involved, except between myself and Fintan of course. But the three of us were inseparable, although I was aware of an undercurrent of jealousy from Fintan towards Erik. Fintan and I were privately tortured about the decision we had made to get married, but when we were with Erik, we forgot our worries and life became about laughter and music. Because we spent so much time together, Erik witnessed his fair share of fights between the two of us, and when it came down to it, he was totally against us getting married.

I was drinking a good bit in those days too. The macrobiotic obsession had fallen by the wayside, because you couldn't get a bag of brown rice in Galway, never mind fucking *hiziki*.

Fintan's mother passed away a few weeks before we were due to walk up the aisle, so there was the funeral to get through, and Fintan was in an even darker place. Although I became embittered towards him in later years, I look back on Fintan now, and see how vulnerable and lost he was, barely twenty-one and taking on so much responsibility: a pregnant girlfriend with her own troubles, marriage and all that entailed, a widowed father. It's no wonder we were having those fights, no wonder he was angry and drinking.

We loved each other, we wanted to be together, but we didn't want to be together in this terrible, trapped way.

The week before our wedding, I had another miscarriage. Part of me was worried about whether I would ever be able to carry a baby to full term, but mostly I felt relieved not to be pregnant anymore, that we didn't have to get married for the baby after all. But my mother had other ideas. When I got out of hospital, I went to stay with her to recover for a couple of days. I told her didn't want to go ahead with the marriage, but she said: 'You have to. It's all organised and you know you love Fintan. It's just nerves, that's all. You'll be grand.'

Two nights before we were supposed to walk down the aisle, Fintan and I had a dirty, violent fight outside a pub on Dominic Street. It was pouring out of the heavens and freezing cold. I was shouting at him, telling him I didn't want to get married to him. 'I don't want to fucking marry you either,' he screamed at me, and we started laying into each other.

I loved Fintan and I hated him. I was clinging to him like a lifebuoy, yet I was battering him away from me at the same time. I think it was the same for him. At the time it felt like hell and heaven, fun and horror, anger and laughter, all at the same time. We were each other's escape, yet we were caught in a trap at the same time.

He stormed off and left me sitting on the footpath in the rain, bawling my eyes out, blood pouring from my nose. A guy I knew called Seamus Kelleher came by on a Honda 50, told me to hop up on the back and brought me to Salthill. Patsy McGarry cleaned me up and, together with a crowd of his friends, gave me tea and sympathy. I stayed up late in the night, talking to Patsy, trying to come up with a plan of action.

The next morning, I went up to Shantalla and told my mother about the fight. 'It's just nerves,' she said, and made me a cup of tea. 'Wait and see, once the wedding is over, the two of you will be grand.'

Erik arrived at the house and saw my face. 'Please don't do it,' he said. 'Don't marry him.' My mother was standing at the sink, her lips sealed, as Erik begged me not to go through with it. When she left him to the front door, they had a talk in hushed voices in the hall, me sitting at the kitchen table like a zombie. I was absolutely lost.

We were married the following morning, on 25 January 1974, at St Joseph's Church in Galway. I wore a blue-and-yellow gingham, floor-length frock, and I carried a bunch of daffodils, my outfit inspired by the Daisy Lady dressed in blue and yellow from my favourite Tir na nÓg song. I had a little job in a boutique owned by a woman called Antoinette Buckley at the time, and she let me borrow the dress from the shop for the day.

It was bitterly cold, and my poor mother had an awful time getting the daffodils I had insisted upon. Looking back, it's telling that my mother also bought the ring. Neither myself nor Fintan had even thought of it, we were so distracted. She got the ring from Fallers jewellers, a beautiful thing that fifteen years later I wrenched off my finger in Dublin and fucked into the Liffey.

The wedding was small, nobody could afford big dos in those days. Angela was my bridesmaid and the whole family was there, except for my grandfather in Donegal, who had passed away by this time. Erik was there, Catherine Geraghty, and some other close friends. We had the reception in the Oranmore Lodge Hotel, with the usual speeches and all that. For me, the whole thing passed in a kind of blue-and-yellow gingham haze.

After we left the Oranmore Lodge and all the older relations had gone home, we carried on to a big party in town, organised by our friends. Both of the Gerts were there, Erik, Nhoj, Paul Hanrahan, Mike Gallagher, Mary O'Malley, Cindy and John, and all the gang. It was a great old shindig, and it marked the beginning of a happier period for myself and Fintan. The wedding was over and done with, we'd gotten through it together by the skin of our teeth, we were back in the bosom of our extended family of friends, and we were setting out on a new journey together. It might not have been a journey to Greece and India, but it was an adventure of its own sort.

Instead of a honeymoon, we went directly to our first home together, a two-bed flat on Maunsells Road that we had arranged to rent, ready for when we were a married couple and could move into it. Erik would be taking the second bedroom, and when the wedding party had finished, the three of us sat up all night on the marital bed, drinking a bottle of Bols Genever, which is aged gin from Holland. It was Erik's wedding present to us, and I still have the beautiful stone-like bottle to this day. Drinking 'til dawn, the three of us began our new life together.

Our stay in the flat on Maunsells Road was short-lived. Although Erik was known as a musician around Galway, he had a sideline creating enormous chess sets, on black-and-white boards made from resin. Instead of the usual horses and castles, his chess pieces were based on body parts. The king was a rather impressive life-sized erect penis modelled on Erik's friend Pietje's penis, which they made a mould of with plaster in a milk carton, while a girl tickled Pietje's balls to keep him erect. The queen was a woman's breast, the castles were pairs of lips, the knights were fingers and all the little pawns were nipples. There was a great demand for Erik's chess sets in

Galway and I know some people who still have one, but for us they had another function. Every time a chess board came into the country, it was filled with bits of hash, which we all enjoyed. Customs were far more interested in the chess pieces than in the board itself, which concealed the Afghan or Nepal or whatever you had in those days.

But as time went on, Erik became more and more worried. And rightly so. Dope may have been legal in Holland, but Ireland was a different story. We decided to move out of the city, to go somewhere quieter, where Erik wouldn't feel so freaked out about the growing number of random callers who wanted to partake of a recreational spliff or two.

So began our chalet lives. The first chalet we lived in was on Gentian Hill in Knocknacarra, about fifteen minutes drive from Galway city. The place was given its name because it's one of the few places in Europe where gentian violets grow.

From the moment we moved in, the chalet was a like a bus station, with people coming and going all the time. A long, hot summer stretched out before us, and we were all perfectly happy. We drew the dole and worked for under-the-table pay for extra cash, gathering clams and mussels for McDonagh's Fish Shop. Nights of music and wine, sitting under the stars in the back garden, were as regular as clockwork, and with Erik's chess sets, those of us who smoked weren't short of a joint or two as the evenings rolled lazily by.

Then, one day, the police arrived, looking for Erik. At that time, Ireland wasn't part of the EU, so if you were non-Irish, you had to register at the police station with your passport if you were staying for anything longer than a holiday. The cops were only there to check on Erik's passport, or so they said, but it was the straw that broke the camel's back.

That night we broke up the very last chessboard with a sledgehammer and buried all evidence in the back garden under a Rowan tree that had been given to myself and Fintan as a wedding present. We rolled a few joints, and Erik and I had a little smoking ceremony in the moonlight, saying goodbye to that phase of our lives. Not long after that, he returned to Holland for a short while.

Autumn was setting in, and because as sure as night follows day, a harsh, cold and damp Galway winter would soon be upon us, we knew that we had to move from the chalet on Gentian Hill. It was a draughty, unheated place that was heaven on a summer's day, but would freeze the balls off a brass monkey on a cold night. We heard that a woman called Mrs Ford was renting out a chalet up the road that was much more insulated and habitable for the winter. It turned out to be in the same group of houses where John and Cindy lived, so we went to take a look and liked what we saw.

By the time Fintan and I had settled in to our own little chalet, without Erik, I was pregnant again. I wasn't in the least bit phased by the news. I was a married woman, after all. We went back to macrobiotics and I started living the healthy life again: no drink and no drugs.

Over the next few months, we became part of an alternative community of like-minded people who were living in the area. Fintan and I were as poor as church mice, but it wasn't a problem. In those days, work didn't intrude too much on us. Most of our socialising was done going to each other's houses.

Mick Fraser and his new American girlfriend, Cathy, lived in another chalet, as did John and Cindy. Fintan was writing poetry all the time and our fights were not as frequent as they had been before we were married. I thought that maybe the worst was over us, that we were learning to be together in harmony, although at the bottom of this was always the niggling worry that we were living a life neither of us really wanted.

When I was six months pregnant, I got the bus into town one day to do a bit of shopping. On the way home, when I stepped off the bus at Knocknacarra Cross, a car came hurtling around the corner and ploughed into me.

People who saw the accident told me later that I flew up into the air and then came down head first into the windshield, before being thrown onto the ground. The wife of the man who was driving found my glasses on the back seat of their car.

I was unconscious briefly. When I woke up, there was a man looking down over me, a doctor who lived nearby. I whispered: 'I'm pregnant, I'm pregnant.' He told me to try and lie still, that we just had to wait for the ambulance to come any minute now.

Fintan came running down the road. 'I can't feel my fucking legs,' I told him.

'Everything is going to be okay,' he repeated over and over again.

Inside, I was pleading: 'Let the baby be all right, just let the baby be all right.' I started saying my Hail Marys.

8

'Tom Traubert's Blues'

When I woke up again, I was in casualty, strapped to a board. Because I'm almost congenitally blind and can see hardly a thing without my glasses, everything around me was just a blur of movement and light. I started screaming: 'My baby! My baby!'

My pelvis was broken, my knee was shattered and my skull was fractured. I had stitches everywhere, but I had not lost the baby. For the moment, that was all that mattered.

Still strapped to the board, I was put into a bed on the Long Ward, with twelve other people on it, where I spent the next ten weeks, only able to move my head and my arms. Two things happened early on that stayed with me well beyond my time in hospital.

Fintan told me that when he was running down the road to Knocknacarra Cross, where he could see me sprawled out on the road, it had flashed through his head for a moment that all his worries were over.

All he was doing was being honest about what was going on

inside him, and it was a brave thing to say, even if it was the wrong time to say it. But I didn't hear it like that. What I heard was that he didn't want us, either me or the baby. This was a stick I would beat him with many, many times over the course of our marriage. I could not let it go.

The other thing that happened was that I became a child again, to all physical intents and purposes, and my mother took on the role of parent in a way that reminded me of the best things about her when we were kids. How she was unstinting in her love for us, how she could take care of the little details. In the years since her pregnancy with Martin, when the change for the worse happened in our household, I had felt alienated from her, and my encounter with her over the abuse in my childhood had left me bitter about her in my heart. But now I was seeing the lovely side of my Mammy again, and feeling comforted by her.

Every day she came to see me and, because I was so into the macrobiotics, she cooked for me so I wouldn't have to eat the hospital food. Ma's version of a macrobiotic meal was mashed potatoes with onions and butter, because I had always loved that growing up. She brought it to the hospital in a flask, so that it would stay warm, and fed it to me because I could not feed myself. I felt very, very grateful to her for it.

Erik came to the hospital regularly too. He would bring his guitar, and sit by the bed playing for me. He told Fintan and me that he was writing a piece of music for the baby.

There were no scans in those days. There was no way of finding out if the baby was all right. My mother and I both had a strong feeling that it was a girl, and if she managed to make it into this world, I was going to call her Aoife, after the first woman, Eve. Mammy said she would bring me in some wool so I could pass the time knitting. Because I hated pink and the traditional thing, Mammy said: 'Okay, well, can I get green and yellow?'

I started knitting tiny socks, and booties and jumpers, even a little sleeping bag, as if with every knit one, purl one I could make my baby all right again, stitch her back together.

I talked to her all the time, not out loud, but inside. If she could just make it through, I felt that she would be born with my whole life story running like the blood through her veins, because she was part of me. And I was part of her.

At night I would get the terrors. The woman in the next bed passed away and I began to think that would somehow have an effect on the baby. I was afraid to go to sleep, because I thought I would never wake up and my little girl would die with me.

One afternoon, when Mammy was feeding me, she said: 'I had a dream last night that your baby was a rabbit.'

'How the fuck could you tell me something stupid like that, when you know that I'm so freaked out?' I snapped, but she thought it was kind of funny that I had a little bunny rabbit running around the place. In the long days that followed, lying on that bed, her bunny dream invaded my thoughts, becoming an irrational fear.

Of course, I know now that my fears were all to do with the fact that I hadn't a clue if my baby was damaged from the accident or not, not to mention the fact that I was going through post-traumatic stress. But at the time, I wondered if I was actually going mad in the head.

Mammy taught me how to crochet and I was working intently on a yellow matinee jacket, when a man walked up to my bed. 'Good afternoon, Mrs Coughlan, my name is Professor Meehan,' he said. 'I read about your tragic circumstances in the newspaper, and I'm here to help, if I can.'

Mr Fergus Meehan was a private consultant at the Galway Maternity Hospital. 'They've told me that you're very worried about the baby, so I would like to examine you,' he said.

He had a heart monitor with him with a little loudspeaker attached to it, and when he found my baby's heartbeat, he let me listen to it. Tears of relief rolled down my face as I heard the tiny thump-thump of it.

'You know what?' Mr. Meehan said, 'I'll leave the heart monitor here with you, so you can listen to your baby's heartbeat any time you like.'

As he left, he told me I would probably have to have a Caesarean because my pelvis was shattered, and he offered to be my gynaecologist, free of charge. I will never forget his kindness.

After I had been in bed for six weeks, the nurses finally allowed me to get up. No amount of begging or whinging would convince them to let me up before that.

I put my feet down on the ground, stood up, and my legs just crumpled under me, leaving me lying there. It took me a few days to walk again. A physiotherapist would come and do exercises on my legs and I was given a Zimmer frame, so I could walk up and down the ward, practicing my steps.

I was discharged three weeks later: over eight months pregnant and unable to walk without the assistance of the frame. I went to Mammy's house for a couple of days' recovery, but more than anything, I wanted to be back in my own chalet. I had been away from home for almost two months.

In the last month of my pregnancy, I was as happy as Larry. Fintan had a job tooling leather for people in Galway who had a leather shop. Cindy would come into me every day with herbs to drink: rosemary tea for strength, blackberry tea for my immune system. My landlady, Mrs Ford, came in every day too, helping me with whatever needed to be done. She was wonderful.

Aoife was born at 7.20 p.m. on 2 January 1977. Fintan was at work when my waters broke at 4.00 p.m. that day, so I shouted down to Mrs Ford, who brought me into the maternity hospital. My mother was a cleaner at the hospital at the time, so she was there when I went in. She was beside herself with excitement, and went off to call Fintan at work, so that he could come in.

The labour pains were worse than I had imagined, but, as any woman who has given birth will tell you, there was an elation there too. They say you forget the labour afterwards: otherwise, the human race would have been wiped out a long time ago, because nobody would ever get pregnant again.

My baby was a healthy six pounds and fourteen ounces. I didn't have to have a C-section after all, so she was born naturally, without the help of any drugs or painkillers whatsoever. Mr Meehan was there throughout, and I felt in perfectly safe hands.

With Cindy's help, I had it all planned out. I was going to

put Aoife to the breast right away. I just couldn't wait to get my hands on her.

The nurse lifted her up to take her away and clean her and I said: 'Oh no! I want to clean her.' I was a bit psychotic. It's a high I've felt every time I've had a baby since. I suppose it's just the hormone surges and weird stuff going on in your body.

Breastfeeding was not the done thing at all at the time: everyone was bottle-feeding. Cindy had no babies yet, but she knew it was the thing to do because she was American, and I trusted in her fully, despite the nurses telling me I was doing the wrong thing. When I breastfed Aoife in those first few days, I would be put out into a little room at the edge of the hospital, in case anyone should see me. God forbid that anyone in Catholic Ireland should come across a woman with her tit out, doing what comes naturally to all human beings.

Mammy took care of me in Shantalla for a couple of days, and then it was back to the chalet, which had only cold running water. I'll never forget the buckets of nappies at the back door: there were no such things as disposables in those days and we all used terrycloth nappies. Mrs Ford, God bless her, used to wash them for me in her washing machine and then dry them out. I couldn't have managed without her.

About a week after coming home, Aoife started crying, and she cried and she balled for the next two months, while I carried her around the house in a papoose strapped to my front, because I was still on the walking frame. She would never let me leave her down, ever, and I was constantly feeding her. I began to have an understanding of what my mother went through when I was her little 'Mary, Mary, quite contrary'.

Erik came over with a basic recording of the song he wrote while I was pregnant. He had called it 'Aoife'. When Aoife was about two months old, he went back to Holland and recorded the song with his band, and it changed his life. It became a huge hit in Holland, making Erik famous overnight. It's been recorded many times in the intervening years and I have a lot of albums with different orchestral arrangements of it.

Nobody had ever talked about postnatal depression in those days. I certainly hadn't ever heard of it, but for a few weeks after the birth I was in a bit of a dark place. Like most new mothers, I wasn't sleeping at all, and I was finding it hard to cope. I was always worried about the baby. I remember putting mirrors up to her mouth at night to see if she was breathing. The rare times she slept, Aoife used to sleep like the dead, and instead of getting some sleep myself, I'd be awake, fucking looking at her.

During the day, I couldn't get around without the walking frame, and I couldn't set the baby down. I wanted to cook dinner for Fintan every day when he came home from work, trying to be the little wife. It all got too much for me very quickly.

Mick Fraser's American girlfriend, Cathy, would come over in the morning times, when Fintan had gone to work. She was fascinated with the baby. One day, while she was goo goo-ing and gaa gaa-ing over Aoife, I burst into tears. I was inconsolable. 'Man, you've got postnatal depression,' Cathy said.

I said: 'What the fuck is that?'

'It's the baby blues,' she explained. 'Women get it all the time.' The next morning, Cathy brought me over a Bruce

Springsteen album, *Born to Run*. I put it on and cried my fucking eyes out for about two hours, listening to the lyrics on it, and then I felt a bit better. There was some proper release. After that, Cathy became very important to me, and her visits helped me get through the blues.

About a month after she was born, Aoife developed this livid red rash that wouldn't go away. She was clearly really uncomfortable and unhappy, crying more than usual. I took her into the doctor, who asked me to put her on the table so he could examine her. As Dr Glynn started undressing her, taking off the layers of clothes I had put on her, he turned to me and said: 'Mrs Coughlan, what the hell is your baby wearing?'

I had been dressing her from head to toe in all the little things I had knit in the hospital, without any cotton vests, and then putting her in the sleeping bag I had made. She was too hot, and the wool was scratching her delicate baby skin. The rash soon went away when I got her more suitable clothes.

Despite the fact that we had a beautiful new little girl, Fintan and I had become distant from each other once more. Back then, I think he was full of blame for me, because he felt that he would never have the life that he wanted. His best friends, Liam and Marty, were living in Paris, having a great time and he was stuck in the backend of Galway with a depressed wife and a crying baby.

We began to argue about his father again, who had made the solemn decree that Aoife would not be let over the threshold of his house because she was not baptised. He wouldn't even touch her. This made me angry as hell. How could the soul of something so innocent, born of nature, so precious and beautiful, be blackened with a man-made thing called original sin? I felt that my father-in-law was trying to control us, trying to make us do what he said by making Fintan feel guilty, but I steadfastly refused to have Aoife baptised. The controversy was big in both of our families for a time, with meetings between the two clans to try and resolve it, and there were daily arguments between myself and Fintan over it.

In the end, we did as we had done when we got married, and Fintan and I capitulated and had Aoife baptised. We only agreed to it when my father-in-law was diagnosed with skin cancer. When the diagnosis was put in front of us, we felt we had no choice but to give in.

After the baptism, when Aoife was six months old, Erik came back to Ireland for a little while, with his new wife, Antoinette, or Anto, as we called her. His song 'Aoife' had gone to number one in Holland, Belgium, Germany, all over the continent in fact, and he was so excited.

He would come over to our place regularly and bring the guitar out, and the singing would begin. A friend of Fintan's cycled down to the chalet one day with Tom Waits' album *Small Change* under his arm. 'Listen to this,' he told us, out of breath. 'It's fucking brilliant!'

And it was. In particular, the track 'Tom Traubert's Blues' spoke to me. The melancholy sound of Waits' voice, the way he lent such depth of feeling to the lyrics. Erik loved the song too, so he learned it on the guitar. I learned all the words and it became our party piece for a good while after that, whenever Erik was in Ireland. When he played while I sang those sad, wounded lyrics, something would happen deep inside me, something that I can only describe now as love. I loved Erik. Singing with him was a special thing: I had a connection to him through music that I have never experienced with anyone else in my life since. When we were making music together, our friendship moved onto a level only the two of us could reach.

In November, when Aoife was nine months old, Fintan and I set off on our big, long-awaited adventure, hitchhiking around France and Spain with the baby in the buggy. I wanted to do it while I was breastfeeding, so it would give us more freedom.

John and Cindy gave us a parachute to use as a tent, so the only thing we had to find whenever we got to a campsite was a big stick to put the thing up on.

I remember being lost in Bordeaux and us having a big argument at the train station, when this man came up to us and said: 'Can I be of assistance?' I had lost the address of the person we were going to stay with, a woman called Florence Caillaud, who had stayed with us in Galway.

As it turned out, this man knew exactly where Florence lived in Bordeaux and he brought us there, first of all stopping at his house to introduce us to his wife and kids and to give us a drink of water.

From there, we went down through the south of France and northern Spain, Fintan picking grapes to make a bit of money, while I took care of the baby. One evening, we set up camp in a field in a place called Burgos on the Pilgrim's Road to Santiago de Compostela. It was quite a cold and windy night in late September, and I was sitting in the darkness, feeding Aoife, when a gust of wind came along and blew the tent away.

I was sitting there with my tit in the child's mouth, screaming like a banshee, and Fintan was running all over the field looking for the tent. It was gone. Forever.

It was really quite hilarious: the two of us ended up laughing hysterically. We were wandering around the campsite with our sleeping bags and the baby in the buggy, not knowing what to do next. These people in a Volkswagen van had seen the whole thing – they were from New Zealand, I think – so we hopped into the van and travelled for a few days with them.

Our holiday was pure freedom, but we had to go back to real life eventually. At the end of November, we returned home, and began to immerse ourselves further into life in our unorthodox little community.

We developed a food co-op, which brought brown rice and wholefoods, the kinds of thing we wanted to eat, into Galway. None of us had much of anything. Our main form of socialising was going to each other's houses for dinner, with all the kids in tow. We spent a lot of time playing with the children, cooking up big pots of food and coming up with plans for the co-op. One day a week, I went to look after the co-op. I would make pasties and cakes, selling them to earn us a little extra money.

I went back to the macrobiotic life, wanting only the best food for Aoife's start in life. I breastfed her until she was fourteen months, when I became pregnant again. There were sporadic fights between Fintan and me about money and drinking. Briefly, we moved in with Fintan's father because he was dying.

I came across a book called *Birth without Violence* by

Frederick Leboyer, and became convinced that terrible pain and suffering was caused to a baby during birth. I didn't know how was I ever going to make it up to Aoife, but I would definitely not let the next one be brought into the world in such traumatic circumstances.

I decided that she would be born in the dark, with a tub of water, surrounded by love, peace and harmony. Fintan would be there and we would all be happy as pigs in shit. I went back to Mr Meehan and brought the book with me, saying: 'Did you know most trauma in a person's life is caused at the moment of birth?'

'What the hell are you on about, Mary?' he asked and I said, 'I want my baby to be born in the water.'

He was really angry with me, absolutely incredulous, saying: 'You want me to put on a wetsuit and bring you out to LeisureLand and deliver her in the swimming pool? No way, Mary. No way.'

When I became well-known later on and went back to Galway to do my first big gig, Dr Meehan bought the very first two tickets that went on sale. He was sitting in the front row with his wife and a big bottle of champagne under his arm all night, to give me after the show. He was really proud of me and I have never forgotten him.

The health food co-op produced a magazine called *In the West*, more a pamphlet really, covering all things alternative and healthy, and I began to write a little column for it about breast-feeding and natural childbirth.

A nun called Sister Stella contacted me through the

magazine. She wrote and said that she had lived in South America with Indian women for years and that there they gave birth in totally natural circumstances and it was much less traumatic. She offered to deliver the baby for me in the Bon Secours nursing home she worked at in Tuam in as natural circumstances as possible. This was over thirty years ago: nothing like that had ever been heard of in Ireland.

With her dark, kind eyes, Sister Stella reminded me of Sister Pious. She had the softest skin I've ever touched and a gentle speaking voice that would lull you into a sense of security. She was unable to find a birthing tank, so the compromise was that no artificial lights would be used. There would be no drugs, nobody would speak and it would otherwise be perfectly quiet.

In his book, Leboyer specified that you didn't cut the cord when the baby was born. Normally they lift the baby's butt and cut the cord and hit them on the back. But when Olwen came into the world, she was put on my stomach and remained there until the cord stopped pulsing and she took her first breath. Her eyes were huge and darting here and there, looking all about her.

It was seven o'clock in the morning in November, so it was darkish outside and there was just the natural autumn light in the room. It was beautiful. Fintan was there, and when the cord was cut, he gently carried her over to a big bath and put her in the warm water. He held her head, and her little arms and legs were swimming around, with her still looking about everywhere. I felt closer to Fintan in that moment than I ever did. For all our arguments and the underlying unhappiness in our marriage, we were as one when it came to things like this, to alternative ways of living and bringing new life into the world.

The Bon Secours nursing home became known for natural childbirth after that. Lots of hippies went there to have their babies in the following years, but our Ollie was the first one.

To further ease her way into the world, we had discovered this thing called baby massage from an Indian woman, coincidentally called Shantalla. Our friend Liam flew home, having found the gardenia oil I sent him chasing around Paris for, and in the first weeks of Olwen's life, I massaged her from head to foot with this oil. I was welcoming her into the world.

Around this time, a guy I knew called Ollie Jennings was part of a group of people trying to get a festival of the arts off the ground. He asked me to pitch in, and we had meetings in my kitchen for the first Galway Arts Festival. I was becoming involved in the cultural side of life and beginning to feel fulfilled, a 23-year-old mother of two with things going on on the side, a whole new world built up around me.

In 1979, because of the huge unemployment figures as well as a lack of national school teachers in the country, the government introduced a new scheme, whereby unemployed graduates, who had Bachelor of Arts degrees, could go to St Pat's in Drumcondra, Dublin and do their special teaching degree. You would be paid three-quarters of a primary teacher's salary for the year, which you would then pay back to the government from your wages in the first three years of teaching. A job was guaranteed on graduation.

Fintan applied for the scheme and he got into it, meaning

that we had to pack up the family and move east. We rented a place on Church Street in the seaside town of Skerries, nearly twenty miles north of the city, and settled down to a new life. It was supposed to bring us a better future, but Fintan's return to college turned out to be the beginning of the end of our marriage.

9

'The Double Cross'

Skerries was an hour and a half on the No. 33 bus from Dublin, and every morning Fintan would go to college and leave me behind with the children. He had entered a new world, where he was learning and making friends: I was stuck and friendless in what I considered was the most miserable fucking bastard place on earth. I was jealous of him, and angry at being left behind: the 'little wife' syndrome again.

Ollie was a tiny baby and two-year-old Aoife was jealous of the new arrival. Ollie was a quiet little thing, so quiet that sometimes you would forget she was there. Once when I was breastfeeding her, her big eyes looked up at me and widened in silent, surprised pain. Aoife was standing at my knee and she had bitten into Ollie's foot, through her babygro, drawing blood. I let a roar out of me, with the shock, and the three of us ended up bawling with fright.

We were poorer than we were back in Galway, where we had most recently moved into Fintan's father's house and hadn't had any rent to pay, so there was little in the way of money to entertain myself. The endless days were spent walking up and down the beach in the freezing cold, just to get out of the house with the two children. I had never known the level of loneliness I felt then. There were millions of women like that all over the world, desperate housewives, they call them nowadays , but it was just such a shock to my system at the time that I had no perspective on it.

I was still in my strict macrobiotics phase, so I would get up at six in the morning and make this porridge stuff we used to eat, before Fintan left at seven. If I could afford it, I would take the long bus journey into town with the girls, and go to a place called the East West Centre on Crow Street, where I could buy macrobiotic food and meet like-minded people. Skerries was utterly bereft of hippies.

The only two friends we had nearby were Paul and Eleanor, who lived in Dublin. We would go to their house, or sometimes they would come to our house, and we would eat together. They had little kids too.

Fintan began to stay late at college and to go in to do assignments at the weekends. He made a new female friend he kept going on and on about. I began to get suspicious and even more jealous. Although I figured, because his new friend was married with small children too, maybe they weren't having an affair.

To ground myself, I took up Tai Chi, bringing the kids along with me to the classes. Unfortunately, if Aoife saw the teacher, a man, coming anywhere near me to adjust my position, she would set off screaming at the top of her lungs and all the other people in the class would look at me accusingly. So that didn't last very long.

Then I turned into my mother for a while, and started making clothes for the kids like a madwoman. I knitted jackets and jumpers and hats and gloves for them, beautiful things. I sewed dungaree dresses for them, and little skirts and tops. Anything to fill the time and give me some sort of purpose in life.

I had become a big fan of Ian Drury, who had had a big hit with the song 'Hit Me With Your Rhythm Stick' a couple of years earlier. To cheer myself up, I bought myself a ticket to a gig he was doing at a place called The Olympic Ballroom in the city. I had the whole thing planned out. I would express some milk into a bottle and Fintan would be able to feed Ollie, and I would get Aoife ready for bed before I left.

But I timed it all wrong. The No. 33 bus terminated at Abbey Street, which was a good half-hour walk in the rain from The Olympic Ballroom. By the time I made the concert, I got to see about four songs and then I had to leave because the last bus to Skerries would be going in half an hour. That was the only night out I had for the entire year.

Fintan was seeing more and more of his friend. My suspicions that they were having an affair started to deepen. Maybe I was just going around the bend by myself with the two children in Skerries, my mind running away with me, I don't know.

There was a large Irish bank on the corner of Church Street, across from our house, and the window at the side of the building used to be open during the day. There was nothing then like the security they have around banks nowadays. I used to regularly think about sneaking through that window, robbing the bank, and just shagging off with the kids, leaving fucking godforsaken Skerries behind, and Fintan too. I was getting more and more unhinged.

Thank God we were only there for a year, long year that it was. At the end of it, Fintan was offered a job in Galway and we moved home to his father's house.

While we were away, Liam had met a woman called Julie, who was from England. Originally, her parents were from Connemara, and she had moved back to Galway to go to college. She was an extraordinary, happy little bundle of energy; I have never met anyone like her and the two of them, Liam and Julie, were head-over-heels in love.

We all shared the house together; it had three bedrooms and two sitting rooms, but with the two kids, it was a bit cramped. When we discovered that I was pregnant again, we decided to sell up.

I had slipped right back into my alternative community of Galway friends. Erik was coming and going. He was so famous in Holland by now that Anto, his wife, couldn't handle the reporters and journalists: she hated all media coverage, so she had moved back to Galway with their daughter, Ana, and bought an enormous house and ten acres of land. At the time, she was also pregnant with their son, Tom.

Pietje and Julia were still around. John and Cindy had a baby called Megan, by this time. I was as happy as I could possibly be to be in the thick of it again, slotting back into meetings about the Arts Festival, the food co-op, and going to lots of big dinner parties in everyone's houses, with all the kids running around.

Fintan and I were out walking one evening, and we saw a

little cul-de-sac of houses being built on the edge of Lough Corrib, looking out over Menlo Castle. We got talking to a labourer who was working on the site. He told us that twelve detached houses were going to be put up, and two of them were going to be at the bottom of the road, nearest the lake: Lakewood Park the development was called. He gave us the name of the builder and we immediately called him and, with the money we had got for selling Fintan's father's house, put a deposit on one of the houses at the bottom of the road, right on the shores of the Corrib. With Fintan's wage as a teacher, we figured we would just about be able to pay the mortgage and survive from month to month.

While we waited for the house to be built, I grew bigger and bigger, full sure the next baby was going to be a boy. As with my pregnancies with the other two children, I didn't drink, or if I did, it was only one glass of wine. I volunteered that July with the Arts Festival; I remember having to pick up Paul Durkin from the train once and bring him down to a reading in Headford School. I had a little green Post Office van, which we bought for seventy-five quid. We had taken the metal out of its side, and put in windows and two seats for the kids. I learned to do my own mechanics. When the spark plugs got damp, I would put them under the grill to dry out.

I got a job in a little knitting workshop on Shop Street, run by a designer called Linda Taube. She lived with a Russian artist called Alex Sodkovski. He painted, and she worked the images he made into these unbelievably intricate jumpers. I used to go down for a couple hours a day and have a few cups of coffee with the other women who worked there, do some knitting, and get paid while I enjoyed the last months of my pregnancy. It was always great craic in Linda's studio and I worked with her for a good few years.

Eoin's birth was natural, in that I didn't take any painkillers or even gas and air. I wanted him to have the best possible start, but I wasn't as obsessive about Frederick Leboyer's ideas on childbirth as I had been when Ollie came into the world. My first son was born in Galway Regional Hospital, and from the very beginning he was a sweet, placid baby, who was smiling at us in no time flat. His appearance in the family took a bit of the heat out of the rivalry between the girls, because both of them were united in their adoration of their little brother.

When our own new house was built, once Fintan's father's house sold, I was very sure of the way I wanted it decorated. I would have cork floor tiles throughout downstairs, and I picked out beautiful Laura Ashley wallpaper, dotted with the tiniest little cherry every so often. We did one wall of the kitchen in it and I made curtains to match, and that room became the heart of our new home.

I thought I had it made. I was a teacher's wife with three lovely children and a gorgeous new house on the lake. So what if my husband was drinking a lot, so what if we were fighting more and more? That was a normal part of marriage, wasn't it?

Having my granddaughter, Aoife's little girl Meíni, around these days reminds me of the chaos of having small children, and the joy in that chaos. I didn't have a great relationship with Fintan, but, looking back on it, some of the happiest days of my life were spent dragging the three kids around Galway. I was twenty-four and I thought I was ancient! I knew that I didn't want any more babies, but I didn't have any more specific plans than that. Life was just playing out the way it was and going with the flow of it felt fine.

My sister Angela had married and had two children, Aoenghus and Niamh, and we would congregate in Shantalla on the weekends, the whole house full of the sound of playing children again. It was like Disneyland up there: Mammy had bicycles, swings, rocking horses – everything was given to those grandchildren. My mother took to being a grandmother like a duck to water and the children all adored her.

My father had been a teetotaller for all the years of my childhood, wearing his Pioneer's pin like a hero's medal, but when he was fifty, he started drinking. Nobody really knew why he took to the booze, but it got bad quite quickly.

When Daddy had drink on him, he would become tortured with regret about how he treated us when we were children. He would arrive to my house in the middle of the night, crying and begging forgiveness for what he had done. It was a pain in the arse, but slowly the hatred that had frozen my heart against him began to melt, until I came to a place of forgiveness.

Erik took time off from the band and moved back to Galway, and soon I was spending more and more time with him. An ad appeared in the local paper for a talent competition, and Erik said we should enter. By this time, the only singing I had done with Erik in public was at parties in other people's houses and at the odd pub singsong, so my first reaction was to say no. But Erik explained that we would only have to sing two songs, and that we could do plenty of rehearsal beforehand. His enthusiasm began to rub off on me.

Erik enlisted the help of his Dutch friend Pietje, the one who had once modelled for his chess set. Pietje played the bass. We began to practice at the house. Our two songs were Billie Holiday's 'Ain't Nobody's Business' and 'The Beach', which was one of Erik and Anto's own. Everyone around us got into the vibe. There was loads of craic at our house every evening. Friends and neighbours coming and going, sitting outside with guitars and singing away, having a glass of homemade wine, the kids running around: it was a time of bliss.

The morning of the day we were to make our big talent show debut, I went downtown to Switzers and bought this blue-and-white striped cotton frock. I thought it was gorgeous. I wore it when Erik came up to the house in the afternoon for our final run-through and he was like: 'What the fuck are you wearing? You look like a circus tent.'

I nearly died. When I looked in the mirror, I saw that he was right: with the blue-and-white stripes, it looked like my head was sticking out of a big top. I started bawling, crying with the shock and disappointment of it.

Erik went up the road to my neighbour and friend, Freda, and said: 'In the name of Jesus, do you have a black frock, a black skirt, a black – *anything* black?'

Freda enlisted the help of another neighbour, Anne, to come down to the house and give me a full makeover.

I didn't ever wear make-up at the time, and Erik had years of experience in performing on stage behind him. There was a woman violinist in his band, and he had watched the way she painted her eyes with dark make-up so that the audience could see them. So he gave instructions to Anne and Freda, and they got to work on me.

They put me in a slinky black dress with shoulder pads and a sort of black lace top over it. It was not something I would wear, normally – I was holding on to the hippie look – but it was good. A pair of high heels and shawl completed the outfit. My hair was backcombed in true eighties style, the make-up was slapped on, and when I looked in the mirror, I was like: 'God Almighty, who the hell is this?' It was like some TV makeover that you'd see today. I absolutely loved the new me.

Fintan was not so impressed. He didn't want me to do the talent competition, so while everyone else was excited about it, he wouldn't get into the craic at all. In the lead-up to the talent show, we had a major fight, in which he accused me of having an affair with Erik. I told him that was a crock of bullshit, and to fuck the hell off if he didn't like what he saw. I was doing the talent show with Erik, and that was it.

I really loved Fintan, and I know he loved me. But the truth was, we were together for all the wrong reasons. If we had been older, more mature, I would have said, the marriage is over, it's finished. I would have done something for myself. But we felt stuck with each other.

The talent competition was at Whisper's Nightclub in Salthill, every Monday night. It began with loads of acts and, as the weeks went on, these would be whittled down, kind of like they do in *The X-Factor* today. Only, there were no judges: you won on claps. The louder the round of applause you got, the nearer you were to the big prize.

So it meant getting loads of people out there to cheer you on. That first night, loads of the friends we had made over the years in Galway showed up and went wild for us. I don't remember being nervous before going on: to me it was just having a bit of fun. Winning was not on my mind.

When we were called out on the stage, everyone went wild. It was so overwhelming, I can hardly remember a thing about it. We had practiced and practiced this routine with 'Ain't Nobody's Business'. In the middle of the song, Pietje dropped the bass, came over and we did a little tango dance, with a rose and everything. It was as tacky as hell, but everyone went mad for it.

We ended up going back every Monday after that until the final, learning new songs during the week, new routines. I was having the time of my life. When it came to it, we didn't win. A ballad singer called Martina took the top prize, after singing 'Silver Threads among the Gold'. The audience, mainly made up of our friends, was gobsmacked. I threw my runners-up trophy on the ground and gave it a swift kick, while the crowd stamped their feet, booing and hissing.

I was not deterred. There was a jazz band who played the pub scene in Galway at the time. They did Sunday afternoons in O'Reilly's in Salthill and Wednesday nights in The Cellar. Erik encouraged me to approach them about singing with them. It would give me good practice at performing in a different situation, getting used to other musicians, new audiences. The band was up for it, so every Sunday and Wednesday, I would do three Billie Holiday standards, 'Nobody's Business', 'All of Me' and 'Lover Man'. I never got paid, but that wasn't what it was about. I looked forward to it in a way that I had not looked forward to anything in my life.

The Sunday morning sessions in Salthill were great fun. Everyone in the family would come: my mother and father, all the kids. It was a really friendly affair.

Wednesday nights were a different thing. Fintan put his foot down about it from day one: he wasn't letting me go. We lived a few miles out of town, and he would do everything in his power to stop me from getting to the venue. One night, he refused to let me go in the car, so I hopped on the bicycle and off I went in the wind and the rain. Hell would freeze over before he stopped me.

All week long, in between the Wednesday gigs, there would be horrific rows. Me screaming at Fintan: 'I'm going to do this. You're not fucking stopping me, you jealous bastard.' Him roaring back, calling me names and accusing me of not caring about the children.

He became like this whole other creature and it would have been unbelievable, if only I hadn't experienced almost the exact same thing with my father when I was younger. As I saw it, Fintan and I had simply slotted into well-defined roles. He had become the father, unable to cope with me taking some freedom for myself now that I was growing up and out of our marriage. I had become the belligerent teenager who was going to do whatever the fuck I liked, whatever the consequences.

The rows got worse and worse. One night, as I was pulling out of the driveway, he wouldn't let me close the door of the car but kept trying to pull the car back as I put it into reverse. I remember the three kids standing in the doorway of the house:

four, three and two years of age, the light in the hallway behind them, just looking at us. I remember their little faces.

Fintan held onto the car door of the car as I tried to get away, and it broke off. I screeched out of the driveway and drove off into town with no door, I was so determined to go.

When I got home that night we had the mother of all screaming matches. I'll never forget that night and it was fucking hard, but I continued to defy him. That's what he said: I was defying him.

During this time, we got some other gigs, supporting the likes of, for example, Maura O'Connell and Honor Heffernan, when they came to play in the Druid Theatre in Galway. In the dressing room after supporting Honor, I couldn't get over the size of her make-up box, with all its pull-out shelves filled with brushes and blusher, and little drawers of every eye shadow colour in the world. 'Jesus, that thing's fantastic,' I told her.

'You'll never need anything like it,' she said, which in my innocence I took to mean that I didn't need loads of make-up to enhance my beauty. 'Thanks,' I beamed, delighted with myself altogether. When she left the dressing room, Erik was fuming. 'She wasn't giving you a compliment,' he said.

Years later, Honor came up to me at an after-gig party and we had a bit of a laugh about it.

Anyway, with the Druid Theatre support gigs, there was a small bit of a buzz around us in Galway. We became friendly with a girl called Siobhán McHugh, who worked as a research assistant at RTÉ in Dublin, and she said we should record a demo cassette and she would run it by Shay Healy, who was then presenting a radio show called *Sounds Promising*.

Defying Fintan's edict that I absolutely couldn't go, I left the kids with my mother and went to Dublin with Gerrard Coffey, who was replacing Erik on guitar when he wasn't available, and a guitarist called Declan Gibbons. A student sound engineer there produced a demo for us free of charge. There were three songs on it: 'The Beach', 'Meet Me Where They Play the Blues' and 'The Double Cross'.

'The Double Cross' was written by Fintan. Erik introduced it to me before we recorded the demo, saying: 'Fintan has written a song. It's about you and it's for you. Will you take a look at it?'

I was like: 'Where is this coming from?' Our marriage was on its last legs, we were having horrific fights all the time about me going out singing, and yet here was a song he had written for me. It was scrawled on a piece of paper and it was about our year in London together, beginning with the image of me going out to work as a street sweeper. I suppose we knew each other better back then, in what I remember as our golden time, but it was all quite forgotten now. He really got the essence of me, of us, in that song. 'Lost without the double cross of you,' it goes, about being lost with someone and lost without them. I found the experience of recording it a bit of an emotional rollercoaster.

It's the only song Fintan ever wrote and it's one of those numbers everybody loves. People still ask me to sing it. For years I used to make a joke that I wouldn't do it, so he wouldn't get the fucking royalties.

Shay Healy liked the cassette and decided to air all three tracks on his radio show. The day he was lining the songs up for play later that evening, who should walk by the studio but Gay Byrne, who is a notoriously big jazz fan.

'Who's that?' he asked, and Shay said: 'It's a mother of three kids in Galway, singing the blues.'

A few weeks later, I got a call to say I was lined up to go on *The Late Late Show*.

10

'Strange Fruit'

On Valentine's night 1982, Fintan and I were invited to a party on a boat down on Galway docks. There was great music going on and at some stage, a handsome American guy asked me to dance. I was flattered and delighted with myself, a 27-year-old girl who never got attention from men like this anymore, but I said: 'Sorry, I can't. I'm married.'

He said: 'Man, it's only a dance. C'mon, you know you want to.'

So I gave in and we went out on the floor. All of a sudden, Fintan was beside us, yelling at the top of his voice: 'What the fuck do you think you are doing? That's my wife!'

All hell broke loose, Fintan screaming at the man, me screaming at Fintan, the man looking like he'd just walked into a scene from *One Flew Over the Cuckoo's Nest*. When Fintan and I got home, the fight got dirtier with him hurling all sorts of accusations at me and me trying to defend myself, telling him the truth, that I had never cheated on him. If fights had been heated in the past, this took it to a new level. It was after that fight when we decided to see a counsellor. When we met our counsellor, Bob, I said, 'I think I just want to leave.'

'Let's try to save the marriage first,' Bob said. 'You have three children and you have invested a lot in keeping it together. It will be a ten-week course: I'll come to your house every Friday afternoon.'

So, for a while, on Friday afternoons, the kids went to my mother's house and Bob came over. In the middle of his time with us, he said we put him back on the cigarettes. He had been off them for a couple of years and now he was buying a box of twenty on the way to our place every Friday, it was that stressful.

He had private meetings with each of us, and counselling sessions with us both together. One day, when things had descended into the worst anger and insults, he asked if Fintan could find somewhere to stay while things calmed down. He asked him to leave the house.

He moved out, and just like that, our marriage was over. Over the next few months, he came to the house fairly regularly to see the kids in the afternoons, because he would get off school early, but we weren't on speaking terms.

I had a brief affair with the American. His name was Mark, and one weekend we went off to Achill together in my little Post Office van. I remember Jefferson Airplane playing on the tape recorder, driving around the island, walking on the beaches and staying in a little B & B. Although it was little more than a lovely, lost weekend, I think the time I spent with Mark restored me in a sort of way. I had felt so old, so battered down by everything that had happened in my young life, but in that moment I was a girl again, free as a bird, with all my life ahead of me.

With Mark gone back to wherever he came from and Fintan gone from the house, I settled into a happy period on my own with the kids. Erik was coming and going, Pietje and Julia were always around, Freda and Anne next door popped in and out, and my life was continuing without all the tension and shit. I felt free to do as I wanted.

By the time my scheduled appearance on *The Late Late Show* was coming up in March 1985, I was a different woman. Money was tight, but I felt like a huge burden had been lifted.

At that time, an appearance on *The Late Late* was like a golden ticket to the big time. Most people in Ireland only had two channels, and the entire country, young and old, sat down on Saturday evenings to watch Gay Byrne host the most talked-about live television show in the land. It was a huge deal for my family that I was on it, and they all came up to Dublin: my mother, my grandmother, my sister Angela. Mammy and Granny were very impressed that Bishop Eamon Casey was going to be a guest on the same night.

I sang my song, 'Meet Me Where They Play the Blues', and then Gay did something he hadn't done before. Unscheduled, he walked over and asked me to come and sit beside him at his desk. Bishop Casey had to move down a seat.

Gay asked me a little bit about myself and then he said: 'Will you sing us another song, Mary?'

At a bit of a loss, I said: 'Well, we haven't practiced any-thing . . .'

'Ah sure, just give us a few bars of something by yourself,' said Gay, so I closed my eyes and sang 'Strange Fruit'. I remember studio lighting dimming and the cameraman moving closer. I had learned to sing my own version of this song in private, but I had never aired it in front of an audience before.

I remember the hairs standing up on the back of my own neck, as 'Strange Fruit' came out of me in the *Late Late* studio that night, Gay silently gazing at me. It was a perfect, unrehearsed moment. When I was finished, I opened my eyes and the studio audience was completely silent, and for a split second I thought: 'Oh man, they fucking hated it.'

And then they went wild, roaring and clapping. Gay was clapping too, and just beaming. He loved to create a good television moment.

The next day the Cork Jazz Festival called a friend of ours, Christy Dooley, in Galway to find me and offer me a gig the following October. He cycled up to my grandparents' house and told them.

I don't know when I saw Frank Miller for the first time, he seemed to be suddenly part of our social group, but I do know that I initially got talking to him at a dinner party in a friend's house, the same friend who had had the boat party on Valentine's night.

We talked about this and that over the night, and I thought he was really lovely, a gentle, caring guy, one million miles away from the jealous, possessive, controlling bastard I had come to see Fintan as. We started seeing each other casually. Frank lived in Dublin, where he worked as a photographer for the *Irish Press*, and he would come down to Galway for the weekend every now and then. I remember being afraid to walk around Galway with him because I was terrified that Fintan would spot us.

Fintan was sharing a house in Salthill at the time. We were not on speaking terms, but he did come to see the kids, mostly in the afternoons after school. He came to the house unscheduled one Saturday morning, and Frank was in the kitchen having a cup of tea. He had just arrived down from Dublin and I was going to bring him into town to show him the farmer's market.

My heart nearly jumped out of my mouth when Fintan walked into the kitchen. I was very scared of him, despite my bravado, and as I expected, he went bananas. There was a huge brawl, the children in the background, with Fintan screaming at Frank: 'Get out of my fucking house!'

In the end, somebody called the guards. They came and asked Fintan to leave, and that was the real end of me and him. He could just get a fucking one-way ticket to Timbuktu as far as I was concerned: I wanted nothing to do with him anymore. From that point on, Frank and I started really going out together.

Over the course of my adult life, I seem to have attracted men who wanted to control me, who were initially drawn to me because I was fiery and opinionated and independent, but who ended up not being able to stand these things about me because, I suppose, it undermined them. There have been only two exceptions to this rule: my current partner, John, and Frank Miller.

The kids absolutely hated Frank in the beginning. Ollie even beat him with her little fists, kicked him in the shins and told him to get out of the house. They had been exposed to so much violence and rage, they were showing it themselves. I didn't understand it then, but I can say it now: I didn't do the right things by my children in those years and for a lot more years to come.

Erik came over one day, sat down at the kitchen table, and said: 'You are really, really good, Mary, and you should be out there. I think we should make an album.'

I had no idea how to make a record, what it cost or what was involved. The only time I had been in a recording studio was when we made the demo for Shay Healy, and that was a very basic affair. But we had a lot of songs together, well-practised and arranged, so it seemed like a natural progression. Erik, who had made several albums already, said we needed musicians to flesh out the sound of the album. We also needed to find a studio and set out a schedule. There was lots to be done before getting down to recording.

While Erik began to make arrangements for it all, I did a few more local gigs. Gerrard Coffey, who had a day job as an accountant, continued to stand in for Erik, while Pietje played bass. Sometimes, when Pietje couldn't be there, Gerrard and I would perform as a duo. Along with the money from these gigs, I was able to put food on the table by working with my uncle Christy, who was a painter. My job was to scrape the varnish off window frames in the houses he was painting. I knitted in Linda's workshop, I cleaned offices three evenings a week and I rented out a room in the house.

Whenever I had time, I would go to Erik's house in

Oughterard and we would rehearse. Sometimes I would have the kids with me, other times they might have been at school or at my mother's. One afternoon, I was driving home from rehearsals with Eoin in the back of the car. It was a Citroën 2CV, a yellow convertible that ran like a sewing machine and was about as solid as a biscuit tin. There was a bit of a back-up on the Moycullen Road, as a woman was waiting to turn right, with a car behind her and me behind that one. I was in a world of my own, singing one of the songs we had been rehearsing, when a huge car came belting around the corner behind me and ran straight into the back of my Citroën, which ploughed straight into the car in front of me. Eoin was thrown into the front – these were the days before baby seats and safety belts – and for the second time in my life, my whole body impacted against a windscreen. The man who ran into the back of us was a neighbour of my mother's, and had been out fishing.

I remember very little of the aftermath of the accident. Eoin was perfectly fine, and I was brought into hospital and given some stitches. After having survived fully intact being knocked down when I was pregnant with Aoife, car accidents were like water off a duck's back to me. I didn't think about my bad luck for even a minute. The next day, a little sore all over, I returned to my everyday life of rehearsals, work and bringing up the children. But the full significance of this event in my life would not come to light for a while yet.

I was invited to do a gig supporting Freddie White, who was a big star in Ireland, at the Olympia Theatre in Dublin, and because Erik was away, Gerrard came to accompany me. We got a great review in *The Irish Times*, and we couldn't believe our luck. There was a momentum building. We could all really feel it.

To record the album, Erik booked a small studio in the middle of nowhere, outside Headford in County Galway. It was owned by the manager of the bank in Headford, who was big into country music – Gerry was his name. We used to go out there in the evening after work and we'd record until midnight. The picture on the back of the album is of me sitting with the crew, having dinner. We would buy bread, cheese and ham in the local shop.

There was a budget of £2,000 for the record. Gerrard had a bit of cash, so he invested some of it and Erik put up the rest of the money. He was producing and playing guitar, Gerrard was also playing guitar and a guy called Carl Hession replaced Pietje on piano. Pietje didn't feel confident enough to be on the album.

Johnny 'Ringo' McDonagh, who had in fact lived across the road from me when I was growing up in Shantalla, played percussion on an overturned rubbish basket and bones. Another guy I knew from Ashe Road, Michael Belton, played the drums proper. Jimmy Higgins played trumpet. And there were more.

The first song we recorded was 'Seduced'. Erik decided that we needed double bass on it, so Greg 'Curly' Keranen from Jonathan Richman and The Modern Lovers, who just happened to be in Galway at the time, was enlisted to do the honours. I was pretty star struck with him because I had Modern Lovers albums in my collection. From a school, we were able to borrow an old double bass, though it had a big crack at the bottom of it. Erik had to lie on the ground and hold it together with his arms while Greg played. It looked more and more insane every take I did.

A friend of ours called Johnny Mulhern wrote 'Delaney's Gone Back on the Wine'. Erik decided that it should be done in an old-fashioned ballroom kind of style, so he drafted in this old guy called Tony Chambers, who back in the day had his own orchestra that played the Ballroom of Romance and the Warwick Hotel when my mother and father used to dance there. Tony was a total character. I don't think he could quite believe we were actually making a record. He played saxophone on the track and at one stage, while he was giving it socks on the sax, he forgot he was wearing earphones and threw himself forward, pulling the amp off a shelf behind him in the process. We all pissed ourselves laughing, including him. He gave the song a sound all of its own. I've never heard anything like it on an album, before or since.

A lot of the other songs on the album were ones we had rehearsed and done at the talent show and in subsequent gigs: 'Ain't Nobody's Business'; 'The Tango'; 'The Beach'; 'Lady in Green'.

Looking back on it, I hadn't a bloody clue what was going on. The first time I walked into the studio, the sound engineer asked me if my cans were all right and I thought he had just said something rude to me. I think my ignorance of the whole business was something that added to the album. There's a raw quality to it that works with the songs and my voice.

Frank Miller took the photographs for the cover: the one on

Mammy and Daddy on their wedding day. Mammy made the cake and the dress.

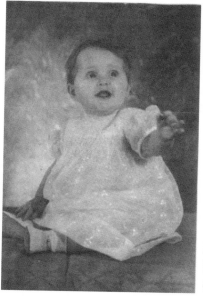

Baby Mary, the best child in all of Galway.

At only a year apart, and dressed up in Mammy's matching creations, there wasn't much telling Angela (left) and myself apart.

My first day at school. No sign of the wild child I would become.

At Salthill with Mammy, left to right: Carol, Angela, Mam, Ger and me.

In Eyre Square with Daddy, left to right: Me, Angela, Dad, Ger.

On Daddy's epic trip around Ireland. I'm still not speaking!

Group shot outside the church on my wedding day to Fintan, wearing the unforgettable gingham dress that, remarkably, I was actually quite proud of at the time.

My beautiful babies. Above left, me with Aoife at Shantalla.
Right, Ollie. Below, Eoin on his fifth birthday and, inset,
Clare and Cian.

I would make many appearances on the *Late Late Show* (above) over the years, a thing Mammy was always very proud of. Below, Mammy and myself, photographed by Fergus Bourke for the *Sunday Tribune*.

Living it up on stage in Helsinki.

Billie Holiday promo shot, HQ, 2000.

Brian Kennedy walks me in to my wedding to Frank.

Myself and John on holidays in Australia, 2005. Look at the state of us!

the front was taken at a wedding in Sligo. I'm wearing a pair of horn-rimmed glasses from the 1940s, something that would become a trademark with me for a while. I bought about fifty pairs of them in a second-hand, vintage shop called Xanadu in Dublin, and had them fitted with my prescription lenses. People used to steal them, so I always had a replacement pair.

As the work on the album wound down my lawyer, Willie Kennedy, wrote to me, saying that the court case was about to be heard for the accident that happened on the Moycullen Road, when the man ran into the back of my Citroën. When all was said and done, I was awarded compensation of £11,000.

In 1985, £11,000 was a lot of money. You could buy a house outright, a good house, with that kind of money. Willie said to me about a year later, when *Tired and Emotional* was number one: 'It's a pity you weren't famous at the time of the court case – you would have got twice that.'

The Friday I got my cheque for £11,000, I held it in my hand and thought: 'Here's my running away money.' I left the children with my mother and went to Dublin to celebrate with Frank. That night, we were sitting in his house on Chamber Street and we decided to move in together and bring the kids to Dublin. We spent Saturday morning looking through the newspapers, and I saw a house in Howth. We went out to look at it and I fell in love with the place. It had a winding path that ran through a rolling, green two-and-half acre garden, with every flower you could imagine. It stretched down to give a stunning view of Dublin Bay, and there was even a tennis court tucked away in one corner. I said I would take it and paid a year's rent in advance.

It was lunacy. In a matter of a few days of getting all this money, I had decided to move to Dublin, take the kids away from their school, their friends and their grandmother, and start up a new life with a man I had met less than a year ago. I was going from cleaning offices to living in the lap of luxury in a house with its own tennis court.

The night before I left, there was a big goodbye party, at which I got absolutely scuttered. At some stage of the night I went out to the off-licence, and, as I was driving the car the wrong way up a one-way street, the police arrested me for drink-driving. I wouldn't let them do a test on me to see if I was over the limit, and gave them awful abuse. The next morning I marched down to the car pound and stole my car back.

My arrest and eventual appearance in court a year later for drink-driving, stealing an impounded car and resisting a police officer was the first time news about my drinking made it into the public eye. 'Mary Sings The Blues,' the headline in the *Connacht Tribune* went, and my reputation as a hell-raising drinker was signed, sealed and delivered, never to be lived down.

The kids were bawling as we were driving away from Galway. They were tortured about leaving their granny, so I made a promise. 'Every Friday afternoon, I'll pick you up from school, and we'll go to Galway, to Granny's house,' I said. And for a while at least, I honoured that promise.

Years later, when Mammy died, we found amongst her boxes letters that Aoife had written her every week for years. These letters were full of little drawings and stories about Aoife's new pals, about what we were doing, what I was doing. The children sorely missed their grandmother.

When my parents came up to visit the first time, my father was terrified of the house. 'You could be dead and fucking buried up here and nobody would notice,' he said. 'You could be murdered in your beds.' It was kind of isolated up on the hill of Howth, but to me, it was a little piece of heaven.

Not one record company wanted the album. I hocked cassettes around Dublin myself, but nobody would bite. The biggest acts in Ireland at the time were Mary Black and Christy Moore, and when they heard my record, the men in the suits were saying: 'What the fuck is this shit? Irish jazz?' It was a not risk worth taking.

Then one day, my phone rang and on the other end of the line was a man called Jackie Hayden, who managed the magazine *Hot Press*. He said: 'A friend of mine is setting up a record label, and he is very interested in you.'

So a meeting was set up. The friend was Clive Hudson, the Managing Director of Warner Ireland, who had already said no to the album. His new label was to be called Mystery Records and I was their first signing. Erik and I signed a deal with them. Gerrard, who had put some money into Mystery Records, signed too, along with Jackie. Clive did not sign the contract and his name was not mentioned on it. A woman from his solicitors signed on his behalf. We signed away the rights for the album for Ireland and the UK, and would receive 10 per cent royalties on 90 per cent of album sales. Mystery Records retained an option on my next album on the same conditions.

As the album was going into production, Erik advised me to get a band together for gigs. Moving Hearts, who were big in the early eighties, had broken up, so a few of them migrated into my band. Matt Kelligan was playing the drums and Keith Donald was on the saxophone. The bass player was Eoghan O'Neill, and Greg Boland played guitar. A year earlier, I had driven from Galway to Dublin in my little yellow Citroën to see Moving Hearts, and back down on the same night. Now, half of Moving Hearts were in my very own band! Our first gig together was at the Cork Jazz Festival, which I had been booked to do after my appearance on the *Late Late*.

At the beginning of December 1985, we played a gig at The Harcourt Hotel to which four people turned up. Frank and I had gone around Dublin putting posters up in pubs and shops, little A4-sized fliers featuring the cover of the album. At the gig, there were more people in the band on the stage than there were in the audience. I was absolutely mortified and getting through the set was like trudging through muck.

Tired and Emotional the album was released at Christmas that year. By February they were queuing around the block to see me.

11

'I'd Rather Go Blind'

Just before the album went into the shops, Erik said: 'You are going to need a manager, Mary. The way this business works is that you put your album out and then you start touring to promote it: that's how you are going to make your money.'

I approached Ollie Jennings, the friend who ran the Galway Arts Festival. I thought he would be perfect for me, but he said: 'I'd love to do it, Mary, but I just wouldn't have time. But there's a great guy in Dublin, he's just starting out: his name is Denis Desmond. I'll give you his number.'

So I rang Mr Desmond's office and left a message with a girl called Katherine.

The Cork Jazz Festival happened, the gig in the Harcourt Hotel happened, the album was just about to come out, and I was getting desperate for a manager. I rang Denis Desmond's office until I was blue in the face. 'Yes, I'll give him your message,' Katherine would say. 'He has your number.' But he never called.

In the week before the album came out, I did a few

interviews and photo shoots. There were lots of media people milling about, and all sorts of people coming and going in my house. Hair and make-up people, photographers, stylists, journalists – it was all a bit bewildering. I still had myself pegged as a plain old housewife and mother.

When *Tired and Emotional* was released, the DJ Mark Cagney started playing whole sides of the album on his radio show at night. In Shantalla, Mammy would bring the radio to bed with her and when I came on, she'd get so excited that she'd run back downstairs in her nightie and phone me. 'You're on the radio, Mary! Are you listening?'

Of course I was. We were all listening.

The album went straight into the top ten of the Irish charts and suddenly I was the talk of Ireland. Everyone wanted to know me, wanted to interview me or get my opinion. Designers were offering to make me clothes and jewellery. Every time you opened the newspaper, there was a review, or a feature, or a photograph of me. My life was turned upside down.

I started getting offers of gigs, left, right and centre. We did the Harcourt Hotel again and people were desperate to get tickets. I slowly began to realise that if the gigs that people were telling me were going to happen actually happened, there was no way I was going to be able to manage babysitting and all the day-to-day stuff with my children.

I was started doing a regular Tuesday night gig in the Earl Grattan on Capel Street. Moving Hearts had decided they were getting back together again, so Greg Boland gave me the name of a saxophonist called Richie Buckley and a guitar player, Conor Barry, who wound up working with me for the next nine years. My new bass player was Ger Kavanagh, Dave Murphy played piano and Martin McElroy was on drums.

At this time in Dublin, there was a major music scene going down. Bands like Light a Big Fire, The Fountainhead and Blue in Heaven were packing them in. I had this dream in my head that if I ever got to the Baggot Inn, I would have it made. It was impossible to get playing there. So when its owner, Charlie McGettigan, called me one evening and offered me a Wednesday night slot there, I let out a shriek down the phone that I'm sure must have deafened the poor man. When I arrived to do my first gig at the Baggot Inn, there were people queuing around the block.

I was making more money than I ever had, more money than I ever imagined. Hundreds upon hundreds were rolling into my bank account every week. Within a year, my entire life had turned around. Instead of scrimping and scraping, making little bits of money here and there to feed and clothe my family, suddenly I was living in luxury. People were screaming to get into the Baggot Inn to see me every Wednesday, and actually being turned away. Offers of bigger and bigger gigs kept coming in.

Then I got a phone call from Katherine Walsh at Denis Desmond's office. I had nearly forgotten Mr Desmond existed by this stage. Katherine said: 'Denis would like to speak to you,' and put him on the phone.

Katherine told me later that Denis had said to her that morning: 'Did you ever hear of Mary Coughlan?' And she had replied: 'Yeah, I've been bloody giving you her number every day for six months.'

Denis came to see me at the Baggot Inn and I loved him the minute I met him. He was this really cute-looking guy with curly hair and funny teeth. He wore this awful, leathery blouson jacket with puffed sleeves and shoulder pads. It was a terrible thing, but it was like his trademark, and somehow it worked.

After the gig, Denis invited me to come and meet him in his office the next day. His office was on Upper Sherrard Street, over the SFX. Denis was sitting behind a big wooden desk on a swivel chair. He was swivelling away in it while I sat straight-backed with my hands clenched, like I was being interviewed for a job. 'I'd like to manage you,' he said, with a twinkle in his eye.

Cool as a cucumber, I said: 'Okay.'

Erik was on a world tour at this time: he was becoming more and more famous too. We spent hours on the phone and wrote letters the length of novels to each other about what was going on. He was delighted I had finally found a manager.

And so the circus began. The album going to number one in Ireland and starting to hit the headlines across Europe. Travelling around Ireland for gig after gig in the back of a van; selling out three nights and two matinees at the Cork Jazz Festival at Jurys Hotel, playing for 1,200 people at a time; doing every festival on the circuit in Ireland and England; selling out gigs in the Mean Fiddler in London. Tickets to see me there were like gold dust.

I was happy and excited and exhausted, having the time of my life. I started to drink after the gigs with the band. I had my first gin and tonic in the Pink Elephant nightclub in Dublin when I was thirty years of age. I really liked the taste of it, and soon the gins were going down the hatch with the greatest of ease.

I employed two girls, cousins from Howth village called Jackie and Joyce, to mind the kids. Jackie lived in the house when I was working away from home. The kids themselves had settled into life in Dublin and the trips to Galway had become less and less frequent. It was every week first of all, and then it became every month, and then it was just every so often. So when I was touring around the place, my mother would come up to stay in Dublin for a few days.

My father never liked leaving home, but he had decided that he didn't like Jackie and my mother staying on their own in the house, 'where you could be murdered in your bed and no-one would know a thing about it', so he came to stay too.

Denis was my constant companion. He came to all the gigs and festivals, and he was always by my side. Once, when I wasn't feeling well and we had a big gig at the Rialto in Derry, he drove me up there in his Jag, instead of letting me go in the van. When we got there, we discovered that there had been a bomb scare at the Rialto that afternoon. The place was surrounded by British soldiers and ringed-off with white ribbon. After a lot of wrangling, we were allowed to go ahead with the gig, which was sold out. Throughout the proceedings, there were soldiers in the wings of the stage, talking away on their walkie-talkies, which gave me ample opportunity to joke around with the audience.

Denis brought me to London to be interviewed for the cover of *NME*, which he said was going to be one of the most important moves of my career. We stayed in the Columbia Hotel, which has a huge staircase in its foyer. Denis had the idea that when the journalist, Robert Sandall, came into reception, I should sweep down the stairs, wearing my trademark sunglasses and swigging from a bottle of champagne. This was the beginning of my image as a careless boozer being projected in the media, an image I have never fully shaken.

I did a gig at the Mean Fiddler while I was in London that time, and interest was really picking up there too. But I was wracked with guilt when I was away from the children, and as time went on, I was away from home more and more. I was torn. If there was a quiet period at home, I'd be itching to be back on the road again. When I was on the road, I felt so bad for leaving my children behind, I'd be craving to go back home again.

Then I got offered a run of nights at the Olympia Theatre in Dublin. I was always sure to have the kids with Frank at these gigs, and my parents when they came up from Galway, sitting in one of the boxes where the audience could see them. It was very important to me to project to the public this image of happy families. I was on top of the world, everything was perfect for Mary Coughlan.

The Olympia show always began with me being carried out on to the stage on a chaise longue by two gorgeous, big, burly men, a glass of champagne in my hand. It was ginger ale, but who was to tell the difference except me?

'The Beach' was the first song I would sing: I would do a few songs that I was very comfortable with at the beginning, because I would become so nervous before going on stage, I'd vomit. I'd be literally shaking from head to foot.

One night, the band played opening bars of 'The Beach', and when I opened my mouth, nothing came out. I was just standing there, looking at the audience, dumbstruck. Richie Buckley was improvising on his sax like a man possessed, trying to fill in the void.

It's hard to explain the feeling I had. Everything went completely still and glassy. It was as if I was outside of myself, watching myself on the stage and thinking: 'What the fuck is she doing here? Who does she think she is?' It was like I was made of wafer-thin ice: one wrong movement and I would shatter into a million sharp little icicles.

I stood there for three or four minutes, the band all looking at each other in confusion, until finally the opening lines of the song came out of my mouth.

That's when I started drinking really badly. I didn't know where to begin with unravelling my feelings. It was like I was two people. Mary Coughlan the mother and Mary Coughlan the famous singer, and neither of those people could find a place to meet. They were a million miles away from each other.

I was having second thoughts about the music business, yet my life was a hundred times better than it had been before fame came knocking on my door. I had plenty of money. I was doing what I loved best. I was able to take the kids on two holidays in one year. To France, camping, and then to Cyprus after Christmas. We were all incredibly happy, yet I was incredibly unhappy. I couldn't make head or tail of it.

On the road and after gigs at home, I drank to cover the confusion, but to the outside world, I didn't look confused at all. 1986 was the year of the first divorce referendum in Ireland, and because I was a separated woman who fully wished to divorce her husband, I was fiercely in favour of a 'yes' vote. My friends Margaretta D'Arcy and John Arden in Galway had politicised me about the issue throughout the previous year, and as the referendum approached, I shared my thoughts in every press interview I did. So, along with the 'Mary likes a drink or three' image, a counter-image began to emerge, of an outspoken, modern Irish woman who was very much in tune with what was happening and had her own political opinions. I started ending every gig with the slogan 'May divorce be with you!', which always got a great cheer. I guess the people who came to my shows were in the political minority that year since, to my shock and horror, the divorce referendum was eventually defeated by nearly two-to-one that June.

It was a summer of constant work, constant attention and constant personal struggle. I looked like I was having a ball, and for a good bit of the time, I was. Walking out on a stage to thunderous applause made me feel an emotion that is hard to put into words. It feels like love, like the whole world is waiting for you to open your mouth, and whatever comes out of it they will adore. In the moment, you adore yourself too, but when the audience has gone home, you have to face yourself. And I hadn't a clue who I was. Fame had come overnight, and I was completely unprepared. I was as lost as a little girl on the streets in a strange city. Looking back, it's no wonder I began to take the wrong turns.

Denis said we had to do another record really quickly, to keep the momentum up. Again, it would be on Mystery Records, while Warner would distribute. We had built up almost enough material for the album that would eventually become *Under the Influence*, but we weren't ready to go into the studio with it, so Denis arranged for us to do an EP for the Christmas market.

The title track of the EP was called 'Ancient Rain' and it was written by Jimmy McCarthy. The second song on the A-side was 'I'd Rather Go Blind', which was one of the first records I ever had when I was a kid. The summer I turned thirteen, I heard the Chicken Shack version of it on the jukebox in the arcade in Salthill, and after that I would go there and play it every evening. I tried to order it in the record shop, but it never came in, so the people who owned the arcade gave me the record at the end of the summer.

We were in studio mixing 'I'd Rather Go Blind', when I discovered that a version of it by Ruby Turner had just shot to number one in the charts. I was devastated. I had picked my favourite song of all time, and out of the blue somebody else had just done the same thing. Since then, I've had this sort of superstition about telling people about the songs I want to do, about putting it out there. I hate when it happens that someone else records the same song at the same time.

I had started to do 'Strange Fruit' as a final encore at gigs, when people just couldn't get enough, so we stuck a version of that recorded live at the Olympia Theatre on the B-side, along with live versions of 'The Beach' and 'Delaney' from the same gig.

For the *Ancient Rain* EP, I had a new band. Richie Buckley and Conor Barry stayed on board, but the rest of the guys all had other jobs during the day and couldn't put in the time. They were replaced by Robbie Brennan on drums and Dave McHale on piano.

We were in the middle of recording *Ancient Rain*, when Denis arrived at the studio breathless with excitement. 'Neil Jordan wants you to audition for a part in his new movie,' he said.

Neil had just won every award going with the independent film, *Mona Lisa*, and he wanted me to try out for his first big-budget Hollywood movie, *High Spirits*, as Peter O'Toole's co-star. I couldn't believe my ears. Me in a movie with Peter O'Toole? *Me?* When I told my mother, she nearly had a fit.

I read a few lines for Neil and he immediately offered me the part.

High Spirits was a supernatural comedy set in a dilapidated old castle-turned-hotel in Ireland, which is about to be repossessed from its owner, played by Peter. In an effort to save his business, Peter's character decides to spice up the attraction a bit for American tourists, by having his staff pretend to haunt the castle with stage-Oirish ghosts. The castle's real ghosts get really pissed off about this, and when a busload of Yanks comes to stay, they come out of the woodwork, leading to all sorts of shenanigans.

The film also starred Steve Guttenberg, who had just made *Three Men and a Baby*; Daryl Hannah; Beverly D'Angelo; Jennifer Tilly; Peter Gallagher; Connie Booth, who played Polly in *Fawlty Towers*; along with Irish actors Liam Neeson,

Donal McCann, Tom Hickey and Tony Rohr. My part was that of Katy, chambermaid and wild Irish banshee.

In the original script, while romance was in the air for Daryl and Steve, Beverly and Liam, my character was in love with Peter O'Toole's character. So, early on in the shoot, I found myself filming a love scene with the man who played Lawrence of Arabia.

The scene was a complicated one, in which the two characters sing a section of Puccini's *La Bohème* in the library of the hotel, me pouring whiskey for Peter, while he strokes my hair. I spent weeks in singing lessons, learning Mimi's song from *La Bohème*, getting my Italian pronunciation perfect, and I worked hard on getting the whole scene right. It was supposed to end with a kiss, and in the rehearsals, Mick Lally acted as a stand-in for Peter. When the scene was finally filmed, the kiss was cut, with the two characters being rudely interrupted, so I never got to kiss Peter. It wasn't all bad though, I got to kiss Mick Lally.

Peter was a great old sport: there are no other words for him. In the middle of filming, he said to me: 'Mary, darling, you are so wonderful. You should lose weight, stop drinking and get a life. You're destined to be a huge star.'

It's a pity I didn't take his advice.

The first part of the film was done in Shepperton Studios over a period of a couple of months. Peter wasn't drinking, but he had the star's dressing room, which came with a bar that was stocked with every kind of liquor you could possibly wish for.

During our time at Shepperton, the Irish cast spent most of the time tucked away drinking in Peter's dressing room, betting on horses and playing cards. We'd be called on set for five minutes, then we'd be waiting around for another few hours, boozing to our hearts' content. In the middle of the day, we'd have huge, luxurious lunches in the studio dining room, with glass after glass of the best of wines. After that, it would be back to Peter's dressing room for an after-lunch drink or three.

This went on every day, and then every night at the Columbia Hotel, where I had elected to stay. I'd barely have rested my head on the pillow, when I'd get a five a.m. call in the morning to drive out to the studio. I'd sleep in the car, sleep in the make-up chair, sleep while getting my wig on. The poor make-up girl was probably getting pissed on the alcohol fumes alone.

The majority of the Americans wouldn't touch a drop. The most I ever remember seeing Steve Guttenberg drink was half of a half pint of Guinness. He lived on vitamins. He carried around bags of the things, and talked constantly to his stock-broker from the phone in the production office.

For all the waiting around, making *High Spirits* was absolutely great craic. Beverly D'Angelo and I became firm friends, and Connie Booth was fantastic fun, always on for all sorts of mischief.

Steve Guttenberg's Hollywood airs got up everyone's noses. I remember one incident, when his girlfriend, a supermodel and apparently the best-looking woman in all of Christendom, was due over. He had this huge bed that he wanted put into his room in Jurys Hotel in Limerick, where we were all staying when we moved there to film on location in November. But the bed wouldn't fit into the room. So Steve asked them to knock the wall down between his and the next room. The manager's jaw nearly hit the floor at that one.

Liam Neeson, who was an absolute gent, also had a girlfriend hanging around. She was this pretty little thing in jeans and cowboy boots, with a big head of auburn hair. Her name was Julia Roberts, but nobody knew a thing about her at that time. She was very quiet altogether, completely focussed on Liam.

There was a terrible division between the Americans and the Irish on the set: apart from Beverly, the rest of the Yanks treated us like lepers. On Thanksgiving night, they arranged a big dinner party and didn't invite the Irish contingent. Peter was deemed good enough to get an invitation, but on principle, he declined and spent the evening with us in the bar at Jurys.

I don't know what time it was whenever I fell into my bed, but it seemed like five minutes later that I was being called to go out to the location set, which was this big castle in the middle of nowhere.

When I got out of the car, my own breath came out in big, thick clumps of fog, it was so freezing. The hangover had really set in at that stage. There was a huge crane beside a bank of trees, and attached to the very top it was a rope that stretched all the way to the castle, a few hundred metres away.

'Now, Mary, today you're going to fly,' Neil said. I looked up at the crane, stretching into the dark sky and my stomach turned.

'No fucking way am I going up there,' I said, but the stunt coordinator was already putting a big leather harness on me. Beverly had made sure that I gave him my exact weight in rehearsals. 'Don't even underestimate by an ounce,' she had warned. 'You don't want that wire breaking because you're too heavy.'

'It's all set up and ready to go,' Neil said, when I protested that I might actually throw up if I had to do it. 'I want you to look at the castle and imagine there are people at the very top window looking at you in horror. We'll set your wire off on the rope and, as you fly through the air towards the castle, I want you to scream at them with all your might.'

So, up I went, hoisted to the top of the trees to wait for the dawn, when they could get their perfect shot. I was so cold, my knees were knocking together, and my head was pounding like someone was battering my skull with a hammer.

Peter arrived on set and squinted up at me. 'Mary, darling, are you all right?' he called.

'No I'm not,' I shouted down. 'I'm fucking dying up here.'

Peter had this guy who was always with him, who he called his 'man'. Throughout Peter's film career, this guy had been his stand-in when they were lining up shots and he was always at his beck and call. So, on this occasion, Peter sent his man back to the hotel to get a 'snifter of brandy for Mary'.

'Now, Mary, drink this in tea, with a lot of sugar in it,' Peter advised, when his man came back with the goods. And up came the brandy tea and all for me to drink, as I was hanging from a crane in a leather harness.

Just as the dawn came, Peter's character set me off flying on the rope, without warning. 'Off you go, Katy,' he said, as the script demanded: 'Fly!'

I screamed like an actual banshee with the shock of it alone, hurtling through the sky at fifty miles an hour. I was absolutely terrified, but that didn't stop them doing it again and again and again, from all sorts of angles. By the time it was finished, I wasn't able to speak, I had screamed so much. My hangover had abated though.

We got a two-week break for Christmas, and I did a few gigs to promote *Ancient Rain*, which was now in the shops. Trying to spruce myself up for my stage appearances, I put a Glintz wash-in colour in my hair, which turned out to be a bit of a mistake. When all were reassembled on set after Christmas, the first thing Neil said to me when he looked at me through the camera was: 'Mary, what the fuck have you done to your hair?'

They couldn't film me, because my hair was a different colour than it had been in the previous takes. So, I was set to washing my hair ten times a day until all the dye came out and I could start filming again.

When *High Spirits* went into post-production, Neil was locked out of the editing suite. It was his first Hollywood movie and he didn't have as much power with the studios as he does now. My love scene with Peter ended up on the cutting room floor, and in the final edit, my part was much smaller.

The moment filming finished, I went into rehearsals with Erik for my third album, *Under the Influence*. In the space of one year, I had released and toured for two records, and made a movie. I had gone from being a single mother who did numerous jobs for a living to a star hanging out with Hollywood legends. The relentless pace of the machine that had been set in motion would prove my ultimate undoing. I wasn't looking where I was going.

12

'Good Morning Heartache'

As 1987 began with the months leading up to recording *Under the Influence*, my drinking escalated. When I was drunk, I was a very difficult woman to handle. Alcohol made me crazy. Not aggressive, but mad as a brush. There were nights when I ran up bills of a thousand pounds, buying rounds for all and sundry in my regular haunt, The Pink Elephant. There were nights when they wouldn't let me in and I threatened to piss on their doorstep, and nights when they couldn't get me out of the place.

Often, at the end of a session, I'd be found curled up in a little ball, crying my eyes out. Denis would get a call in the middle of the night, and he'd get up out of his bed to come and rescue me. I was a nightmare to deal with.

One morning, I woke up and discovered that my car had been stolen. I still had the keys, but it wasn't outside the house. My friend Helen said: 'Maybe you left it in town,' so she drove me around the city looking for it. Eventually, when it was nowhere to be seen, I went into Pearse Street Garda Station to report it stolen, and the guards at the desk just laughed at me.

They had seen me getting into my car drunk and had driven me home instead, bringing the car into the station. 'You invited us in for tea and sandwiches, Mary,' the Garda told me. 'But we declined.'

I was drinking, but I was still functioning, taking much more of an interest in how the new album would play out. Erik and Anto had written new songs that we wanted to include on *Under the Influence*, the songs 'Dice' and 'AWOL', and there were also lots of other numbers like Peggy Lee's 'Don't Smoke In Bed', and Jimmy McCarthy's 'Ride On', that I wanted to record. On this album, as far as I was concerned, every song would mean something to me: there was nothing going on there that I couldn't relate to totally.

There was a story in the news at the time about an ice cream man in the north city who was also a heroin dealer. He would sell the kids a '99' and a bit of smack to their parents. Both Johnny Mulhern and I thought it would be a great story to turn into a song, and that's where 'Ice Cream Man' came from. Johnny wrote it for me, and it is one of those numbers that became synonymous with my name. Elvis Costello once told me that 'Ice Cream Man' was one of the greatest songs ever written. He hoped to someday get the chance for us to record it together.

I became increasingly involved with how the songs would be played on the album. I didn't want 'Good Morning, Heartache' to be recorded as a jazz standard. Billie Holiday was in the throes of heroin addiction when she recorded that song, and I wanted that to come out in my version. So Erik figured out a way of playing the chords backwards, which gave it this delirious, sad quality. It wasn't just recorded and then played backwards: the drums and guitar on that track are actually played backwards. I don't know how he did it.

The new band, like me, were all fond of the drink, and couldn't stand Erik and his perfectionism. 'Herr Flick', they called him. 'I said nine a.m., and it's fucking ten past,' he would say to them if they arrived late for a recording session. 'This studio is costing us a thousand pounds a day, and you're getting paid too much. So turn up when you're supposed to!'

They had all served their time in the music business and wanted to do it in their own lackadaisical fashion, but Erik was a strict taskmaster and it rubbed them up the wrong way. At the same time, they were completely in awe of him because he was such a musically intelligent person.

Under the Influence was released in the summer of 1987. Having moved on from speaking out on behalf of divorce, I was now giving interviews about the desperate situation for the many young women who have to leave Ireland to get abortions in England, and the lack of options and education they had. I wanted to put an abortion referral number on the cover of the album, but WEA were having none of it. No amount of foot-stamping on my part would change their minds, so I had to go with the decision.

The album was an instant hit. Before setting off on a promotional tour, I was invited along with Mary Black and Marion Fossett by the RTÉ Concert Orchestra to represent Ireland with them in the annual radio competition for orchestras in Belgium. It was the first time I would get to sing with an orchestra and I was in heaven at the idea.

We had to do the show in front of hundreds of people and there were going to be radio and television people there from all over the world. It was decided that we would be choreographed, from our walking onto the stage to our steps while we were singing. They brought Joan Kenny, Tony Kenny's wife, in to work with us. She would rehearse our movements with us in the studio at RTÉ. We had to do three of our own songs each and we had to do a medley together, which the powers that be decided should be a collection of Supremes numbers. Joan had us going: 'Stop, in the name of love, before you break my heart. Stop!', and putting our hands out and doing a little dance routine.

Mary was getting into it big time, and Marion was well used to doing routines with her band Sheba, but I was all over the place. No matter how simple Joan made it, I kept fucking it up. Because I was so nervous singing in those days, I used to stand like a statue of the Virgin Mary in front of the microphone when I was on the stage: I would never move a muscle. It was agreed, after much trying to get me choreographed, that Mary and Marion would dance and that I should just sing. In the end, all the dancing in the world didn't matter. The two others were knocked out after the first round.

The whole thing was sponsored by Bollinger. While I would be going on from quarter-final to semi-final to final, I envied Marion and Mary as they toasted me with flutes of champagne, without a care in the world. At least I got to share in the bubbly with them when I won.

Back at home, Denis and I were living in each other's

pockets. His business was going from strength to strength, and now that he was promoting most of the big acts coming over to play in Ireland, the money was rolling in. I remember sitting in his office with him as he did deals with managers for the likes of Huey Lewis and the News and Simply Red. Sometimes I'd be able to bring the kids backstage at concerts and they'd meet their popstar heroes.

Frank and I had a happy thing going together. When I wasn't gigging or touring, or drinking my head off, we had a normal, settled relationship. He was one of Ireland's top press photographers and when my mother was up in Dublin minding the children, I would often meet him after work to go for a few pints in Mulligans on Poolbeg Street, opposite the offices of the *Irish Press*. I got to know all the journalists in Dublin there, something that would stand me in good stead. Many of them showed great loyalty in the years to come.

As I set off across the UK and Europe for the *Under the Influence* tour, Frank stayed behind to help take care of the children, who were eleven, nine and seven years of age at the time. By this stage, I had bought the house in Howth for £135,000, which was a lot of money, but well worth it for the security of having the family there. There were various babysitters on hand for the times Frank was working, including my mother and father. Frank was such a strong and steadfast person and I trusted him absolutely with the children – Aoife, Ollie and Eoin have all grown up to have a good relationship with him – but, at the time, I didn't fully appreciate what he was doing for me, how he was supporting and helping us all.

I was gigging all over the place. Everybody wanted to go see

Mary Coughlan. In London, if you were la-de-da, you went to see me at the Palladium; if you were trendy, you went to Sadler's Wells; and if you were a gobshite, you went to the Mean Fiddler. Every place we played was packed out. Shane MacGowan, Elvis Costello, Nick Cave – singers I had admired from afar – were coming to my gigs, hanging out in my drsesing room. After a gig one night, Van Morrison offered to buy me a cup of coffee. I thought I had died and gone to heaven. Since 'Listen to the Lion' had such an effect on me as a teenager, I had bought every single one of Van's albums, everything he had ever done. And here he was, telling me how much he liked my work. Another night at a gig Ollie thought she had died and gone to heaven because she was standing right next to Morrissey.

It was like one big, long party and I threw myself into it without a thought. I wanted to be away from home, I wanted to be living the high life and part of me wanted to forget I had responsibilities. Nobody else around me seemed to give a flying fuck about anyone but themselves. I partied night after night after night, at home and abroad, and I was hardly seeing Frank and the kids at all.

During this time on the road, I became closely involved with a man whom I had come across regularly in my life as a singer. It was the beginning of an affair that would last a year and a half, and would almost destroy my life and family. It seemed like we were two individuals hell-bent on a common path of self-destruction, and during that time I reached new lows in my life that I had not ever thought possible.

I couldn't tell my story properly without talking about this chaotic, crazed period of my life, not just because of the effect it had on me personally, but because of the far-reaching trauma it caused my three children. I'd only realise the full extent of the damage done to them at a much later stage as I tried to put the pieces of our broken family back together.

Though I was still with Frank, I started spending more and more time with this other guy, and I knew that I wanted it to go further. I have never been a woman to cheat on a man, so I sat Frank down and told him about my feelings. He couldn't believe it. Although he had been living with us in Howth, he had always kept his own house going. Reluctantly leaving the children, he packed his bag and moved home. It took a long time for Aoife, Ollie and Eoin to get over the loss of him, and the arrival of this new man into my life, whom they hated from the outset. Without properly thinking about the consequences, I had destroyed our family unit in one fell swoop.

The kids may have loathed him, but for a long time, I was blind to the truth about my new boyfriend. I really liked the attention that he was giving me: it made me feel special and singled-out. But soon, the attention got so much that he would be standing at the side of the stage when I'd come off, and he would bring me into my dressing room. He began to keep me away from other people.

We drank, and I did a lot of cocaine, which I had taken a bit of a liking to when we were doing the final mix of the album in Holland a few months earlier. Whereas I went a bit all over the place with the booze, a line of coke or two on top of it made me feel clear-headed and sure that I was in the right about all the decisions in my life. We started sleeping together.

I was utterly infatuated with him, even though nobody else seemed to share my positive feelings.

When I look back on it, I realise that I was not taking responsibility for anything in my life. I handed over all responsibility to this guy, and it suited me down to the ground. We lived in this kind of crazy world of our own, and I was cut off from the pain of being away from the children, from the guilt of hurting them and Frank so badly. It was easier to be away from home all the time now, because I was so ashamed. I called on my parents more and more to babysit, while I went on the road.

The guys in the band took me aside and said: 'Mary, stop this relationship. It's dangerous.'

'Mind your own fucking business,' I told them.

We arrived back in Ireland after a month of gigs in London, and in the airport this woman came up to my boyfriend.

'Mary,' he said, 'this is my wife.'

You could have knocked me down with a feather. He was smiling at me, as if this kind of thing was an everyday occurrence, his wife absolutely innocent of the fact that I had just spent the last month shagging her husband.

Did I leave him? Well, the answer to that one is, no, I did not. Instead, I entered into a year of personal torture, during which this man played me and his wife off against each other, and every other important relationship in my life began to disintegrate.

I'm working with the same piano player now as I used to work with in those days, and he still talks about that terrible relationship. 'How did you ever do that, and why?' he asks.

All of the shit things that I did in my life led me eventually, many years later, to the place where I absolutely had to look back and ask the same question. Why did I put myself and my family through such hell? But at that time, I was not able to ask such questions; reason had gone out the window, like a baby with the bathwater. This man brutalised me mentally, emotionally and eventually, physically, and I took it like I deserved it, with my children suffering from the fall-out.

He would stay with me for weeks and then go back to his wife. Then she would throw him out and he'd come back, and I'd take him in. We'd go off on the road touring and we'd be together, and when we got home, he'd go back to his wife. I would be lost without him, then he'd come back. Then we would have a violent row and I'd throw him out, and he'd go back to his wife. And it went on and on like this, with me becoming more and more deranged every day.

I was the furthest thing from a mother to my children at this time, unable to be there for them in any sense of the word. All I could selfishly think about was this man I believed I was in love with.

Before he left, Frank told the kids that he thought I needed help. I hated him for that. I told him it wasn't any of his fucking business, but he said: 'I care for you Mary, and for the kids, and I think you should get yourself sorted out.'

When Frank moved out, my cousin Ann Marie came from Scotland to live with us, and I credit her with taking care of my children's emotional health through it all to the best of her ability. Ann Marie was a wonderful friend to me, and to my children. If anyone kept any sense of normality in my house, it was her. She tried to ground me and keep me sane, even though it was hell for her too.

I had never been one for drinking at home before, but in this latest relationship, I discovered the joys of Tequila Sunrises in the afternoon. We were constantly hammered.

On the road, I was like a maniac, always on the verge of hysteria, absolutely out of control, and it was damaging everyone around me. The same story kept on playing out like the same episode of a soap opera on repeat. Him going back to his wife; me going crazy; him coming back; me throwing him out: and on and on.

One night, in a drunken haze, I decided I would drive over to where he was staying and that, somehow, I would kill the bastard. When I got there, I parked outside, trying to get the courage to go in and do the deed. I fell asleep and woke up with my face plastered to the window and the police tapping on it. 'Are you waiting on the Ice Cream Man, Mary?' one of them asked me, before bringing me home in the squad car.

It all came to a head one evening while we were in Howth. We had both been drinking for hours and I was screaming at him to go back to his wife, telling him I wanted him out of my life. I pushed him towards the door and he retaliated by grabbing my hair and bashing my head against the wall. One of the kids called a family friend, who brought me to the Mater Hospital, where the gaping wound in my head was stitched up.

That was the beginning of the end of it. At least I had the sense to realise that a line that should never be crossed had now been trampled on. I decided to cut him out of my life completely.

But he wouldn't go that easily. My phone began ringing at

all hours of the day and he'd beg me to meet up with him, telling me he had no place to go, that his wife had thrown him out too.

'I don't have anywhere to live,' he would say. 'It's all because of you.'

So I gave him money. On the surface, I didn't want him anymore, but deep down, it was a different story. We were on a constant knife edge between me letting him back into my life and us never seeing each other again.

When I was asked to open *High Spirits* at its premiere in Dublin's Savoy cinema, I decided I would invite him to come with me.

'Are you completely out of your mind?' my friend Beverly D'Angelo said, when I told her. 'If you bring that low-life bastard, I will officially never speak to you again. I don't want that man near you.'

In the end, I took her advice. More for the children and my parents than myself. They were all so excited about being there, so thrilled and proud of me: bringing that bastard would have destroyed the whole thing for them.

For the night I had had a stunning dress made of green silk shot with pink, designed by Sharon Hoey. It had big puffed sleeves and it was so tight, it barely covered my arse. The entire Irish media turned out for the event. As I got out of the limousine and went into the cinema, flashes were going off left, right and centre. It was like a dream, and now that I look back on it, one of the peak moments in my career. It was as if everything had come together perfectly at last. *Under the Influence* was riding high and I had a big film coming out. I smiled for the cameras and did my very best to look every inch the star.

The news that came after the premiere couldn't have been better. 'You might want to sit down,' Denis told me when he called. 'WEA want to sign an international deal with you. They want to do a major new album and release it all over the world.'

It was the opportunity of a lifetime, but it didn't come without a terrible price to pay.

13

'The Whiskey Didn't Kill the Pain'

Erik and I went into rehearsals for the new album immediately. It was such a relief to be back to some sense of normality, looking forward to something new, to starting again with the madness of that crazed relationship out of my life. We would rehearse all day and go out for a few pints afterwards, my drinking soon returning to more normal levels. We were working on some really great songs, like 'Leaning on the Past', 'Hearts', 'Lucy's Dream', 'Pornography': a lot of really experimental stuff that never has seen the light of day since. Erik called the style we were developing 'drunken jazz trad'. No one had heard anything like it before.

In the middle of rehearsals, Pete Briquette and Bob Geldof arrived and said: 'We wrote this song. It's about two junkies, and the band don't want to do it. We think it would be great for you.' I was thanking my lucky stars the Boomtown Rats had turned it down, because to say I loved 'Little Death' is an understatement.

There was another song I had set my heart on: it was called

'The Whiskey Didn't Kill the Pain', and was made up of two songs that John Duhan had sent us. We liked parts of each song, so Erik took the best of each and blended them into one. We recorded a demo duet of it, with myself and Gavin Friday, and included it with 'Little Death' and eight other songs on a tape we were sending to Rob Dickens, the WEA record executive in London.

As part of the new deal, WEA wanted the rights to my first three records, which had been released on the Mystery Records label, but the Mechanical Copyright Protection Society (MCPS), which ensures songwriters are paid their rightful royalties, would not release the albums. Mystery Records was no longer in existence, and none of the original writers on the first three albums, people like Jimmy McCarthy and Johnny Mulhern, had been paid. The MCPS were holding me personally responsible for paying the large sum of money that was owing to them.

WEA said they would pay the money to the MCPS, but that they would then own the rights for *Tired and Emotional*, *Ancient Rain* and *Under the Influence*. Erik and Gerrard, who had co-financed those records, would be paid £5,000 each and once that had been recouped in new earnings, they would be paid their proper royalties. The money owed to the MCPS would come out of my advance for the new album, and I would be paid royalties for the first three records separately from now on. Until all of the money spent on making the new album, plus the costs of making a video for the first single was recouped, I wouldn't make any profit.

'That's all fine by me,' I told Denis, relieved that the MCPS would be off my back, and we travelled to London to sign the contract.

When we arrived at the WEA offices in Kensington, Rob brought us into his office and said: 'The truth is, we don't like the songs on your demo, Mary. We thought that maybe we'd go in a different direction with the new album. Your fan base is getting bigger and bigger, and with the exposure videos on MTV can give you, what's needed is a really good, popular song.'

I didn't really know what to say. I liked all the songs we had worked on, particularly 'Little Death' and 'The Whiskey Didn't Kill the Pain', but I was open to looking at new material. I told Rob as much, and he said: 'That's great, Mary. So, we want to get a new producer on board. His name is Pete Glenister. He had a number one album with Terence Trent D'Arby and we think he'd be just the man for you.'

He continued on telling us about this new producer, but I kind of tuned him out while the penny dropped.

They wanted to fire Erik.

'I'm not working without Erik,' I blurted out, and there was a moment's awkward silence. 'Why don't we give you time to think about it?' Rob smiled, showing me to the door. Denis remained behind.

After a while, Denis came out to the reception area, where I was waiting. 'I'm not doing it without Erik,' I told him. 'They can just fuck off.'

'Why don't you go out for a cup of tea?' he said. 'It will give you time to calm down and think.'

I went into a coffee shop next door, ordered a hot chocolate and sat looking at it for two hours, going over and over the implications of what had just happened. I couldn't do this to Erik, but if I refused to work without him, what would happen?

Denis made the choice very clear when I returned to the WEA offices. 'It's simple,' he said. 'They don't want you if you don't want to do it with Pete Glenister. That's it. Everything you've worked for will be down the toilet. At this stage of your career: all finished, all over.'

I started to cry. 'Look,' Denis said, 'Pete is great, he has just produced a number one album for Terence Trent D'Arby. This is your big chance.'

Telling Erik was one of the worst things I ever had to do. I wrote to him explaining what had happened and the impossible situation they had put me in. I called him and said: 'Erik, I'm so sorry. I'm so sorry,' over and over again.

'I understand,' he said, but he sounded very far away. He had worked in the music industry long enough to know how it operated, but no matter how much he understood, we had been a team for so long that it came as a huge personal blow: he was deeply hurt and very angry.

'All of this is your fucking fault, you know,' I told Denis, even though he had been put in the exact same position as me.

Before recording started on what was to become the *Uncertain Pleasures* album, I started working on Neil's next film, *The Miracle* – a smaller-budget affair filmed in and around Bray and our house. The crew was all the same and my friend Beverly D'Angelo was back in Ireland to star in it. I had a small part as Mrs Stonewall in a stage production, within the film, of *Destry Rides Again*. Throughout the filming, I was feeling incredibly nervous about recording my new album with a producer I didn't even know, and sick to the stomach about having had to go along with getting rid of Erik.

It was being shot in the Gaiety. On the day they were filming my part, I tore into the drink with a vengeance in Neary's Bar between takes, until eventually, mid-shot, I passed out. I was carted off to the Meath Hospital, and the whole sequence had to be cut out. A red-headed double was used for other shots, where they could get away with using the back of my head.

As it turned out, Pete Glenister was a great guy and I had had no need to be nervous. He liked 'Little Death' and 'The Whiskey Didn't Kill the Pain', although he wasn't too keen on the way we had treated them on the demo. A compromise with the record company was reached, whereby I could keep both of those songs on the album if I sang the song Pete had written, the one that was supposed to get me in with the MTV generation. It was called 'Invisible to You', and it was actually a very nice song. Pete also wrote the opening track on the album, called 'Man of the World', which is a great great song.

All the rehearsals and recording sessions for the *Uncertain Pleasures* album took place in London, which meant spending weeks away from the children, who were still being looked after by my cousin, Ann Marie. The London house the record company rented for me was the most beautiful place I had ever lived in, and a new routine was established very quickly.

Pete made me work much harder than I ever had before, forcing me to sing in keys that weren't familiar, stretching my voice beyond its comfort zone. I was working with a new band too: Bob Andrews on keyboards, Christian Marsac along with Peter on guitar, and on drums, both Blair Cunningham, who had worked for Michael Jackson, and Neil Conti from Prefab Sprout. My backing singers, Fran Kapelle and Violet Williams, were to work with me for a long time to come, and Kirsty MacColl came in to sing backing on 'Invisible to You'. We stayed friends for years after that. When she died so tragically in 2000, it was a huge shock to me, and I miss her to this day.

They were all good guys and they had respect for me, something I wasn't necessarily used to, but I was utterly out of my depth. I needed the reassurance of having some people I was familiar with in the mix, so I put my foot down and insisted that Conor Barry and Richie Buckley come over to record with us.

That concession, and the inclusion of my two favourite songs, was about all WEA budged on. In every other respect they called all the shots. This was to be a more *Top of the Pops*-oriented album: I was to become a pop star. One of the tracks we chose was Billie Holiday's 'I Get Along Without You Very Well', which was a song I loved. Singing it was like a message I was sending myself about getting along without Erik very well, but really I was lost without him. It was like I was in a sleek little boat, drifting out to sea without oars or an anchor.

Denis arranged a couple of gigs for me in London when the recording was finished: nothing huge, just a few nights to try the new songs out. I was doing it with my usual Irish band, so I flew home to rehearse with them.

I was coming home from rehearsals one day, pulling into my driveway, when I saw an outrageously beautiful guy walk by. He was tall, tanned, skinny as a whippet and he walked with a certain confidence. 'He can't be Irish,' I said to myself, wondering where on God's earth they grew gorgeous men like him.

I found out the next day, when I went to have a drink with my friend Anne Johnson in the Summit Inn at the top of the Hill of Howth. The same guy was sitting with her when I arrived. Frank Bonadio was his name. He was Californian, from Santa Barbara, and had big brown eyes that just swallowed you up. Years earlier, he had gone out with Anne's sister and he had stayed in contact with the family after they split. He was over from the States, visiting with them for a week.

We bantered over and back for about twenty minutes, and there was a definite mutual attraction going down. Later I invited the crowd back to my place for drinks and Frank came along. When I left him to the door in the wee small hours of the morning, I thought I would never see him again.

The next day, rehearsals were running late, so I rang the kids to say I'd be home in an hour. 'Somebody just sent a bucket of roses for you,' Aoife said. 'It's huge!'

They were from Frank. No Irish man in my experience had ever made such a grand gesture of interest, and it felt very good, especially after the past year of emotional deprivation. I called Frank up at the hotel where he was staying and thanked him.

'I have to go to London in the morning, to do this gig,' I said, and he replied that he was going back to America the day after that. 'It was nice to meet you,' he said before we hung up.

I went to London, did the show, and when I got off stage, he was there waiting for me.

And that was it. After just twenty minutes of casual chat in a pub, Frank became a permanent fixture in my life, deciding not to go back to America for the time being. The kids had met him already in Anne's house, where they regularly went to play, and they were equally charmed. They called him 'the Pied Piper'. When the flowers arrived with his name on them, they must have thought Mammy might be happy with this man, after the terrible time she had had with the last one. They were pinning their hopes on him.

Frank accompanied Denis and me on a whirlwind promotional tour for *Uncertain Pleasures* in the weeks prior to its release. WEA were bankrolling and we stayed in luxurious hotels across Europe, stopping off in country after country, where I would do television, radio and press interviews. In Germany, I did eighteen interviews in one day, while Denis and Frank bonded in the background, becoming great buddies.

In Finland, I was invited onto a television show on the same night as Paula Abdul, who was a big international pop star at the time. The story went that, hearing that she would be on the same programme as another female singer, Paula refused to come out of her dressing room, so I ended up being the star that night. I never even got to meet her.

As the promotional tour wound down, Denis said to me: 'Frank's a really good guy, Mary. Don't fuck it up this time.'

I laughed and promised that I wouldn't.

*

On its release, *Uncertain Pleasures* was greeted with a mixed response. It got great reviews across the board, but my hard-core fans hated it. The video for 'Invisible to You' got plenty of MTV play and WEA had my name everywhere, but the people who had bought my previous albums weren't interested.

My management planned a massive tour, like nothing I had ever done before, stretching across the whole of Europe, from Spain to Scandinavia. First, we did lots of gigs in Ireland and the UK, which were packed out and as popular as ever.

I had an enormous band: fourteen people including back-up singers, roadies: the whole works. Along with our tour mana-ger, Aidan Lee, we spent ten weeks in total on a tour bus, going from one country to another. We'd get out of the bus, do a sound check in the venue, have something to eat, do a gig, have a shower at the venue and then get back in the bus to travel to the next place. It was like being on a treadmill that never stopped turning, except when we had a day off and could actually sleep overnight in a hotel room.

In all this time I didn't get to see the children, and Frank was back living in America. We talked on the phone every day, and I was as torn as ever between life on the road and life with my family.

The whole lot of us on the tour bus were totally out of control, with Aidan Lee desperately trying to keep us together. I can't remember much about the tour. Whole countries passed me by. A few years ago, I did a gig in Denmark and the promoter came up and said: 'That was better than the last gig you did here.'

I said: 'I never played here before.' He showed me photographs on the wall to prove that I had indeed been there.

We divided up into little groups, with myself, Fran and Violet being the female contingent, making our own fun whenever we could.

When we got to each venue, our rider was: one bottle of tequila, one bottle of vodka, one bottle of brandy, one bottle of Gordon's gin, six bottles of champagne, six bottles of red wine, six of white, and six crates of beer. What we couldn't drink before or after each gig, we took on the tour bus with us, and I drank way into the night, supplementing the booze with plenty of coke.

We got two days off when we went to Amsterdam, and they passed in a blind funk of dope smoke. The youngest member of our contingent was our saxophonist, Kieran Wilde, grand-nephew of the great Oscar, and this was his first time away from home. He was like a kiddie in a sweet shop, bedazzled by all the porn and prostitutes waving from their windows, not to mention the coffee shops.

Myself, Violet and Fran went out shopping for him the day before our gig there and, as usual, when the show was finished we all piled back on the bus. Kieran, exhausted after his coffee shop shenanigans, passed out on his bunk and while he was asleep, the girls and I wallpapered pages from porn magazines in his little space. When he woke up, there was a dildo hanging from the ceiling, two inches from his face, flanked by a pair of little red apples.

We played the legendary Roskilde Festival in Denmark, along with other Irish bands: An Emotional Fish and Hot House Flowers. There we hung out with 10,000 Maniacs, who loved a good game of football against the guys from our band, and The Sugar Cubes. Their lead singer, Björk, was preoccupied with her new baby and spent much of her time in the Volkswagen van they toured around in.

Throughout the *Uncertain Pleasures* tour, money was not an object. Whatever anyone needed, they got, no questions asked. In case any of the musicians was unable to go on stage one night, other musicians were paid on a retainer, just to be there to step in.

WEA had put all their money into advertising the album, but they were giving us minimal tour support. I didn't know it at the time, but they thought it was too ambitious a tour. It was too long and went to areas that weren't tried and tested. Having said that, that tour has stood me in very good stead in my career. I can play anywhere in Europe now, and I'll get an audience because of the *Uncertain Pleasures* tour.

I had been told it was a safe bet. I was going to be a huge star and to make sure of that I had to be seen by as many people as possible. WEA's investment might be limited, but the money I was going to make would more than make ends meet: I would be set up for life.

'Do whatever it takes,' I had said when I was first presented with the contract, signing on the dotted line. It never occurred to me that the tour might incur losses, and that I would be liable for those losses. I didn't understand that I had put my home up as collateral.

14

'Sentimental Killer'

Frank Bonadio says he will never forget the look on my face when I walked out of Denis Desmond's office after being told that I had lost everything.

With all the extravagant costs, the tour had been a write-off, and about two weeks after we got back to Ireland, Denis called me into his office to give me the bad news.

All through the years, all the money I earned from gigs and advances went into my National Irish Bank account. I got a payment in cash every week for pocket money. Everything else – my mortgage, my car repayments, my bills – came out of this account. I never looked at a bank statement in my life. I didn't understand until that day in Denis's office that the same account had been used to finance the tour, and that because of this, my mortgage had not been paid for over a year, never mind the car and other bills.

I sat in Denis's office as he and Gerrard explained it to me in black and white. I was hardly able to take a word of it in. I had defaulted on my mortgage, the value of the house was collateral for a tour that made massive losses, and the bank wanted payment. Every single penny in my account was gone. Nissan wanted to repossess my brand new silver car, and I was in serious arrears with my telephone and electricity bills. I owed the National Irish Bank a lot of money.

'What about the first three records?' I said. 'There must be some earnings coming from them.' Up until that point, I had not received one penny in royalties.

'Mystery Records is no longer trading,' Gerrard told me. 'Remember, you have to wait until Warner clears the debt with the MCPS before you see any money from those records. And *Uncertain Pleasures* isn't doing as well as expected.'

I ran out of the office in a blind panic. Everything was gone. My house, my career, everything I had worked for. Frank went white when I told him. He drove me back to Howth, me sitting beside him with my head in my hands, crying: 'What am I going to do? What am I going to do?'

Was it only a year since I had been walking the red carpet into the premiere of *High Spirits*, feeling that everything was just coming together, that I was on top of the world?

'I never liked Howth anyway,' Frank said. He hated my friends there and believed it would be better for me to be out of the place. 'You can sell the house and we'll rent somewhere,' he said. 'You'll be back on your feet in no time.' But he didn't look as if he believed a word he was saying.

In the end, that's what we had to do. That June, a builder bought my stunningly beautiful house on two-and-a-half acres stretching down to a sea view, giving me two months before we had to vacate. We looked for a house to rent and found a three bedroom semi-detached on a faceless estate in Portmarnock.

The day we moved there, I stood in the kitchen looking out at the tiny square of grass out the back, fenced-in by breeze-block concrete walls, and drank a bottle of Southern Comfort from the neck. I could hear the neighbours in the adjoining house talking as I directed the movers to fit our furniture in as best they could. Outside the window, a string clothes line stretched from a rusty pole in the corner of the garden to the back wall of the house, a solitary dish rag hanging on it from a faded blue plastic peg. This was my life now. No more red carpets, no more sell-out gigs, no more audiences showing their love: just a clothes line in a patch of garden for a view day in, day out, and me a housewife once more.

The kids started adjusting to the local school. Frank glued himself to the television to watch the unfolding first Iraqi war, smoking sixty cigarettes a day. For me, life just stopped short.

Within weeks, I began popping into the local hotel after the kids had gone to school for a few brandy and ports, just to get me through the day. Before long, I was falling out of bed and drinking myself into oblivion. It was the only thing I could think of doing. I was in a black hole of depression, and I could see no way of crawling out. I was drinking heavily before the loss of my career, but in those days there had been the structure of gigging and recording to build my alcoholism around. With all that scaffolding gone, the booze was the only thing holding me up.

Since I had come back from the big tour, I had been suffering with really bad stomach problems. Now the pains in my gut were getting worse and worse, and I was suffering from an awful lot of nausea and vomiting. I didn't attach the pain and sickness to drinking: instead I thought I had developed a stomach ulcer from the stress of the past year. I went to a doctor, who sent me into hospital for some tests. When my results came back, the same guy phoned me and said: 'There's nothing wrong with your stomach, Mrs Coughlan, but your liver is in bits. You'd better stop drinking, and stop drinking now. You better get yourself some help.'

I decided to take his advice, and got myself into the St John of God psychiatric hospital in Stillorgan for a thirty-day rehab programme. 'The Stillorgan Hilton', they called it: you could check in and check out, as if you were in some five-star hotel, and there was a pub just across the road. Although there were several people in there avoiding tax or because of drink-driving offences, the majority were going through their own quiet, personal hells. I remember a man whose wife brought him in an orange, full to bursting with vodka. She had syringed it in. Another man's wife collected him to bring him home to the country, and while she wasn't looking, he had filled the windscreen washer under the bonnet of their car with vodka. He insisted on driving and all the way home, he pretended there was something wrong with the engine, bringing the car to a stop every so often, so he could 'look under the bonnet'. By the time he arrived home, he was plastered.

In the midst of all these stories, bizarre as it may sound, I couldn't for the life of me figure out why *I* had ended up in the place. I had checked myself in, yet I didn't believe I should be there. I went to the AA meetings and said all the right things. I spoke to Dr Tubridy, and declared that I wanted to stop drinking. I admitted that I was an alcoholic and did everything that was required of me. I forced myself through the whole process because I thought: 'This is my redemption. This is the way to get my life back in control.'

One weekend towards the end of the month, I was allowed home for a night to see how I would get on in the outside world. When I got out, Frank was waiting for me. Sober and full of relief to be free of the place, I was totally enamoured with him, and he with me. We fell into each other's arms, delighted to be back together again.

I hadn't had a child for twelve years, but over the next two weeks, I became very aware that I was pregnant. I could sense the change in my body instantly, and I started craving tomatoes and salt.

By the time I got out of the hospital, I was as sure as night follows day that I was cured. I was happy to be sober and pregnant, and Frank was over the moon. He decided to give up his job as a bioengineer and move to Ireland permanently. His plan was to go back to college, to do a research project at Trinity College. This was the brand new start we were looking for.

As if to confirm the fact, Denis phoned up and said: 'Guess what? WEA want you to do another album!'

That wasn't exactly true. They weren't exactly shouting for me to do a follow-up to *Uncertain Pleasures*. Their plan to make me a global success hadn't worked out, and they had little or no interest in me any more. *Uncertain Pleasures* was part of a two-album contract, which WEA could have reneged on, but Denis found a way to keep them in the loop. 'Bring Erik

Visser back,' they said. 'She might work better with him after all.'

I had never fully lost contact with Erik. Our friendship might have been strained, but he had been deeply concerned about what had happened to me, and we had spoken on the phone several times.

'I hated *Uncertain Pleasures*,' he said when I called and begged him to come back and work with me again. 'It wasn't you, and it alienated all the people that know you. We need to go back to where you came from musically.'

Full of excited enthusiasm, he came over to Ireland and we started working on the new album, along with Johnny Mulhern. I got a small advance from WEA, and we went into a little studio in Dublin to rehearse some of the songs we had already come up with before Erik was fired from *Uncertain Pleasures*. Johnny was writing away like a mad thing, great new songs like 'The Magdalen Laundry' and 'St Francis of Assisi'. Although there was nothing like the kind of hype that had surrounded the recording of *Uncertain Pleasures*, it felt absolutely right to be back in the studio with Erik. This was going to be a return to the sound we had been building together prior to *Uncertain Pleasures*. We were very confident and fully sure it was the right way forward.

I rang Denis and said: 'You've got to hear what we're doing, man. I think you're going to love it.'

'I'll be in to hear the demo first thing tomorrow morning,' he replied. 'See you bright and early.'

The next day, Erik and I went into the studio at the crack of dawn to set up three or four of the best mixes of the demos we had. We waited all morning, but Denis never showed up.

I was six months pregnant, I was managing to keep my family on a tiny advance from the record company and I was facing letters from National Irish Bank every day, setting up court dates that I kept trying to put off. Having waited like a gobshite for Denis to hear my demos, I was left feeling that he didn't actually give a flying fuck about what was happening to me, despite the fact that he had been my manager throughout the whole fiasco.

We were supposed to be going to London the following day to play the Fleadh in Finsbury Park – an Irish music festival that I had appeared at for the past few years. Darryl, who worked for Denis, told me that Denis had appointed a new tour manager for this, as well as another couple of gigs lined up in the UK.

'Fuck that,' I said. 'I'll manage my own tour. Tell Denis he's fired.' And I hung up.

Before I got on the plane to London, I met Gerrard for a coffee. 'What the hell is going on?' I asked him, but he just sipped his coffee and avoided the question, asking me how the new album was going.

Not long after that, Gerrard, my good friend and long-time associate, moved to America. He sent my accounts on the train from Galway in two Tayto crisps boxes, and I never heard from him again.

From day one, neither Erik nor I had received any royalties for the first three albums on Mystery Records, although they had been sold all over the world and licensed to different record companies in different territories.

I went to London and I did the Fleadh and the Mean Fiddler without a manager. Afterwards, when I got paid £10,000 for the gigs, I was completely dumbstruck. But just as I wasn't aware of the amounts of money I was earning, I wasn't aware of how much I was spending either. In short, I was broke. Well, almost broke. I had managed to squirrel away £20,000 that nobody knew about.

All through the months we lived in Portmarnock, I had my eye on Neil Jordan's house: No. 2 Martello Terrace in Bray. We called it 'Magnificent Terrace'. Its enormous front room stretched the length of the house on the first floor, with French windows that led to a balcony with an uninterrupted view of the Irish sea. The master bedroom upstairs had the same view, so you could wake up every morning to it.

Neil loved Martello Terrace, but his real dream house was a few miles away in Dalkey. I had always said to him that if he ever moved, he had to sell Martello Terrace to me. As he got ready to release his new film, *The Crying Game*, he decided that the time to move was right, and promised me a deal on No. 2, if we did it privately. I managed to get a mortgage for £100,000 and, together with the £20,000 I had stashed away, I bought Neil's house.

Suddenly, I was sitting on my new sofa, queen of all I surveyed in my new mansion, Portmarnock fading into the distance like a bad dream. Somehow I had pulled myself, Frank and the children out of the suburbs and got us this perfect house by the sea. I was hugely pregnant, and, although the place was freezing and in need of new windows and insulation I couldn't afford, I had plans for Martello Terrace. I was going to make it my project, to restore it to its former glory slowly but surely. I was more content than I had been in years. Frank and I were very close; the children were looking forward to the new baby; Erik was back. And I was working every day, singing every day.

Christy Moore's manager at that time, Mattie Fox, had heard that I was no longer working with Denis, and he asked me out to dinner. Mattie was very successful in what he did with Christy Moore, and he seemed straightforward. He had heard through the record company that the new album was going to be a much smaller deal with Warner Ireland, and he believed he could salvage it, now that Denis was gone.

'I'd like to manage you, Mary,' he said. 'I know the MD of Warner Ireland, Peter Price, and I think we will be able to work something out.'

So Mattie became my manager, and it was all systems go again for the new record.

I didn't drink a drop of alcohol all through my pregnancy with Clare, but on the night I went into labour with her, I got a terrible craving for a gin and tonic. I asked Frank to go out and buy me just one, and I drank it, watching a Robin Williams stand-up video with him. I laughed so hard at that video, that when my waters broke, I wasn't sure if I hadn't just pissed myself.

Clare was born on 6 November 1992, in Holles Street. A beautiful, curled-up little thing with a dark head of hair, she had a band on her tiny wrist saying, 'Baby Coughlan'. We had to go to the Registry of Births to change her surname to Bonadio.

The house filled with visitors and flowers. The record company sent bunches of pink balloons and everyone was so happy. The album, which we had titled *Sentimental Killer*, was due out at Christmas, and a tour to promote it was lined up for the following March. The Irish gigs I had no problem with, but already I was wondering how I was going to manage with a five-month-old baby, touring Europe and the UK.

'Don't you worry,' said Frank. 'I'll take care of the baby. All you have to do is get out there, twirl your arse on the stage and bring home the bacon.'

When Clare was six weeks old, we went to America so that myself, Aoife, Ollie and Eoin could meet Frank's parents, and they could meet their new grandchild. They lived in Santa Barbara and we were to stay with them for a week before visiting Beverly D'Angelo in Los Angeles. Neil Jordan was in America too, the toast of Hollywood after the success of *The Crying Game* and already in talks about doing *Interview with the Vampire*.

The first week we were in Frank's parents' house, I got up in the middle of the night and went to the drinks cabinet. They found me passed out there in the morning.

Of course I know now what triggered it, although at the time, I hadn't a clue as to why I had laid into the drink with such ferocity. Frank's mother, however, was wise enough to recognise there was something coming between me and my new baby, something that made me feel like a less than useless mother.

Frank would never set the child down. After I had breastfed her, he'd scoop her up in his arms and take her away. He'd sing her to sleep, he'd change her nappy, he'd walk around the house all day, holding her on his shoulder: he was totally besotted with the baby, and no one else, least of all me, could get a look-in. We had agreed before we left for the States that, when the album was released, he would take care of the kids while I worked, but I didn't realise that it meant I was just going to be used as a breastfeeding machine a couple of hours a day.

'You would want to put a stop to that,' Frank's mother warned me.

After the drinking and passing out episode, Frank got more protective of Clare. Now, not only was it my job to be the breadwinner, I was not to be trusted with my little girl. I understood where this was coming from. Frank had suffered through an extremely bad time with me and had looked out for my children while I just drank myself into oblivion. But the upshot of it was that I didn't get the slightest little chance to bond with Clare, and, coupled with a touch of postnatal depression, I was becoming desperate and I didn't know why. I felt worse than useless in the mothering department, and powerless over Frank's decision to take Clare entirely into his care.

We stayed with Frank's parents for Christmas, and I didn't drink again. The fact that Frank's father had hidden every drop of alcohol in the house helped.

When we got to LA, I left messages for Neil at the Chateau Marmont, but no call came back. We eventually drove to the hotel and walked into the lobby, looking like the Beverly Hillbillies. Neil was out by the pool, but he was preoccupied with some Hollywood A-listers. From the hotel, I called Beverly D'Angelo, who said: 'Never mind that bullshit, come and stay with me.'

Beverly threw her beautiful house open to us and held a party in our honour. The next day, she took the three older kids shopping on Rodeo Drive, and got them clothes and shoes and all sorts of stuff. The kids were completely in awe of Beverly. Frank and I had a lovely time together with her, which made up for the tension between us in his parents' house.

Coming back to Ireland meant facing the prospect of the tour for *Sentimental Killer*, which I was dreading. The morning after we arrived home, I got out of my bed, drove down to the local off-licence, bought myself a bottle of vodka and drank it down in one session. From that day, until Clare was two years of age, I would be hospitalised thirty-two times for alcohol poisoning.

15

'God Bless the Child'

The next two years exist only as a blur in my memory, the whole sorry experience blending into one horrible stretch of self-loathing, self-pity, and some sober periods, where I was trying to cope but thinking of alcohol all the time.

As I drove the people I loved away from me, at the same time I felt abandoned by them. I was clearly surplus to requirements. My children looked to Frank for everything, and he took care of everything for them. I was beginning to pay the price for what I had done to them from the time of that hellish relationship. I was just someone on the sidelines of the family now. I had a baby, I had a man who wanted the baby, not me. And my other kids wanted him and not me.

Deep down, I began to believe that I had made a mistake in getting into a relationship with Frank in the first place. I had that old feeling of being trapped that I had had so long ago, when Fintan and I got married. I had left Fintan, but there was no way I could leave Frank. I couldn't do it to my children again. I couldn't take them away from someone else.

From the point that my career took off, I had hardly been a mother to them. I didn't help them with their homework; I didn't help them growing up; I didn't help them as teenagers. There were nice times, of course: holidays and periods when I was not drinking and everything was calm. But there was a wound in the family, a wound that I had inflicted. To rub salt into that wound would drive them all away from me forever.

After Clare was born, Frank didn't come near me again. He moved out of our room and I felt alone and unloved. But I understood why he didn't want me. It was awful for him. I was drinking myself unconscious, going in and out of hospitals, leaving him to cope by himself with my children and a small baby. I was no support to him at all, and I was a revolting mess.

I was selfish. I drank because all I wanted was to be out of my own pain and misery. Other peoples' pain and misery weren't even blips on my radar.

I felt betrayed by everyone, yet in between the drinking binges, I'd sail along, pretending not to care, making out that everything was just fine. I was doing the same as I always had. All the acting out and running away when I was a kid: that was all to hide a deep pain and bitterness, not only from the world, but from myself too. Nothing had changed in that department.

As far as my career went, Mattie Fox was in the driver's seat, trying to get me sober. The *Sentimental Killer* tour was planned for the summer. We needed the money badly. It was 1993, and mortgage interest rates had shot through the roof in Ireland. We were suddenly having to come up with double the repayments due when we first bought the house. Frank was bringing in hardly any money, and we hadn't two brass farthings to rub together.

Mattie reckoned that the only way I would get through a tour was if I went to a treatment centre for a month before we took off. So, while he got the band and the dates together, I went down to Aiséirí, a private clinic in Wexford, to dry out.

The whole time I was there, I just couldn't wait to get out and start drinking again, and looming ahead was this tour. I didn't know how the hell I was going to manage it.

Before we went on the road, Mattie said that he wanted to talk to me about a few things, our image and that kind of thing. He wanted the band in suits. He knew a dressmaker and he said: 'Time now to get out of the short skirts, Mary, and put on some nice linen trousers.'

I said: 'You can go fuck yourself, Mattie.' I had lovely legs, and I liked showing them off.

Mattie had the band well drilled in keeping me sober. No drink was to be allowed anywhere near me throughout the tour. Of course, as any alcoholic will tell you, that doesn't keep a drinker away from drink. It certainly won't stop you from thinking about it, which is the worst part.

I slipped out of a place one night where we were about to go on stage and Sven, my bass player, came after me. He found me at an off-licence with a bottle of vodka in my hand, guilt written all over my face, like a bold child.

'Give me that,' he said, and I handed it over, giving him the dirtiest look I could muster. He was just taking care of me, they all were. They loved me and really respected me, and they thought they were doing me good.

No good could be done, though. I knew what I wanted and, just as it was when my father was trying to curtail my freedom as a teenager, I was going to get it by hook or by crook.

We toured all over England, ending up in Scotland. The whole thing passed without much incident, until we were in Glasgow. We were waiting to do a show and I was locked into the dressing room to keep me away from the bar, so I climbed out the window and down the fire escape. Halfway down, at the building next door, the fire escape stopped and I had to knock on the window of a flat, where a couple were watching television. They let me go through their place and down their front stairs.

I went out, drank a half-bottle of vodka – down the hatch in just three gulps – and I came back to do the gig.

The whole Scottish side of the family were at that gig, including my Aunt Rose, who I loved so much. I remember thinking, after this gig, I have to talk to my Auntie Rose, I have to tell her what's going on. She'll understand.

Up until that night, nobody used to know I was drunk when I was singing. But this time, we were doing Leonard Cohen's 'There Ain't No Cure for Love', and I was so plastered I lost the words. 'I walked into this empty church, I had no place else to go,' I sang, and then forgot what came next. Kieran Wilde was playing the sax and he kept having to repeat the loop while I sang: 'I walked into this empty church, I had no place else to go,' over and over again. I was stuck: I couldn't get out of the song.

Kieran came over to me, put his hand on my shoulder and said: 'Get out of the fucking church, or I'll stick this saxophone so far up your hole, you won't fucking be able to sit down for a month.'

I got out of the church and somehow got on with the gig.

Back at home, I was sneaking drink whenever I could, doing all sorts of things to fool myself that I did not have a drink problem, like sticking to Mateus Rosé wine, which was like lemonade. Inevitably, the drinking would escalate and when it got to its worst, I would lock myself into a room with just a mattress, a ghetto blaster and a basin to vomit in. I spent hour upon hour in that room, drinking two, three, four full bottles of neat vodka, listening to Frank Sinatra or Billie Holiday singing 'God Bless the Child', over and over again. The only time I would come out of the room was to go to the toilet.

I would lie on that mattress and wait for sleep or complete drunken oblivion. Flashes of my childhood would pass before my eyes. My grandfather kissing me, my uncle masturbating in front of me, my father beating me. But I couldn't delve too far into thinking about it all. If I did, the room would start spinning and I'd get the fear. The fear that I was being sucked into a black hole of shame.

Vodka was the only thing I was living on. I didn't eat. Instead, I started mixing down my vodka with Ribena, for Vitamin C. It was my version of the healthy option.

I would go through stages of being able to keep nothing in my stomach. I'd be able to keep the vodka down without vomiting for ten minutes, and that was enough to give me the feeling of alcohol in my blood.

One time, Frank went to get Dr John McManus, who lived

next door and was always at our beck and call, the poor man. He saw the state of me and injected me with enough tranquilliser, he said, to knock out an elephant. I was locked into the room without any alcohol, and when I came to, I opened the window, jumped down onto the balcony, went all the way across everybody's balconies in Martello Terrace and down the drainpipe at the end. I ended in some pub or other. Later, the Gardaí found me crying on the street and brought me home.

When it got to the point of no return, Dr McManus would get me signed into a hospital, St John of God, or Loughlinstown, or wherever they would take me in. Sometimes I went of my own accord, sometimes I fought, sometimes I was so drunk I wouldn't even know they had admitted me until I woke up in my hospital bed. I would get the fright of my life, finding myself attached to a drip, alone on a psychiatric ward. I'd think: 'Fuck, here we go again.'

Of all the hospitals, St John of God was the easiest to walk out of. I'd be admitted, and two days later I'd saunter out the front door and hitch a ride home in my pyjamas. I stole a fiver in St John of God once. I was wandering around the place with only one thing on my mind, to get out and get a few drinks. I saw a fiver on a locker in one of the wards and there was nobody around, so I lifted it.

I snuck out, got myself a half-bottle of vodka and hid it under my locker. 'That will do me grand for a while,' I thought and went down to the dayroom, delaying the gratification. Next thing there was an announcement on the PA system: 'Would Mary Coughlan please come to the nurses' station?'

Somebody was being admitted and they had needed to fit an

oxygen tank in the ward. The nurses had moved my locker and found the bottle.

They stopped taking me in St John of God after I had been admitted umpteen times, saying: 'This is a place for people who are sick and want to get better, Mrs Coughlan. We can't help you anymore.'

I would emerge from whatever hospital I had been admitted to and take up my life again where I left off before the drinking got out of control, completely sober sometimes for as long as fourteen weeks. Mattie would drive me around to do a few gigs in Ireland, or I might be back in England for a couple of nights at a time, because I had to make money. We still had a mortgage to pay.

On the New Year's Eve after Clare's second birthday, we were invited to a big party in Neil Jordan's new house in Dalkey, for which Tom Cruise and Nicole Kidman had flown in. It was packed with A-list film celebs.

I had a good bit of drink on me, so I was bold as brass. 'You're very small,' I told Tom, 'but Christ, you *are* gorgeous.'

He laughed out loud, and asked me to sing. I sang 'The Beach' for him. Nicole spent most of the night quietly chatting to her sister in a corner, so I didn't get to talk to her. At one stage, I was looking over at Tom talking to Frank. They were like chalk and cheese: Frank, a tall, imposing man, Tom, looking like a shiny, white little boy.

'Frank,' Tom said, a little loudly, so that the whole room turned around to look, 'you're smoking.'

'I know,' Frank replied, 'I'm trying to give them up.' 'No, man, you're *actually* smoking,' Tom said, and we all noticed that the back of Frank's jacket was burning. He'd been leaning back to avoid blowing smoke in Tom's face, and his jacket had caught fire from the candelabra on the piano.

Somebody threw a pint of water on him, and the party continued on in fine style.

When I wasn't working, during the sober times, I would be cleaning. I would get down on my hands and knees and scrub every corner and crevice of the house from top to bottom with a toothbrush. In the kitchen, everything would come out of storage and into the middle of the floor, and I'd be scrubbing the corners of the cupboards with my toothbrush, making sure there wasn't a speck of dirt or bacteria to be found anywhere.

When the cleaning was done, I'd take up redecorating. Into town I'd go, coming back arms full of fabrics of all sorts. I made curtains; I made chair covers; I made quilt covers to match the curtains and chair covers. The kids, when they came home from school, would never know what way the furniture was going to be, or what their bedrooms would be like. The house was in a constant state of lunatic change.

All the days and weeks I was sober, all I would think about was drink. I was going to AA meetings, sometimes twice a day, but nothing worked. During those times I started to buy naggins of vodka and hide them in the sneakiest ways.

One of my favourite hiding places was a lifering on the seafront about twenty or thirty yards from my front door. I would stash my bottle of vodka in the yellow wooden casing, behind the ring, where nobody could find it. I could pop out the back door, run down, take a good long gulp and get back to the house without anyone noticing.

I had other hiding places too, like the metal bin outside the Harbour Bar, or the boot of the car, under the spare wheel. I'd take Clare out for a walk, sneak a bottle from one of my hiding spots, and get a can of Coke at the chipper to mix it down with. I'd sit on the seafront, eating my chips and drinking my vodka and Coke.

I always had an emergency supply at the bottom of the clothes basket in the laundry room, which allowed me to do the family's washing and ironing and get slowly sloshed as I worked.

After a while, when the drinking got worse and worse, Frank would buy me alcohol to keep the peace, and I'd go back into that room, with my Billie Holiday CDs and my self-pity and my self-loathing. I'd drink myself into a dangerous condition again, and be carted off to the hospital again.

Once, when Frank and the kids were trying to get me into the car to bring me to the mental hospital in Newcastle, they were startled by a neighbour and they dropped me. Frank had my shoulders, Ollie and Aofie had a leg each, and between the jigs and the reels, I landed slap-bang on the ground. I can still hear my head clattering off the concrete. We laugh about it now, but it was no laughing matter back then. They just pulled me up, bundled me into the car and got rid of me for another while.

We had AA sessions in the hospitals and I spoke to psychiatrists one-to-one, but I still didn't even think of speaking to anyone about what had happened to me as a child. It was a secret that was buried so deep within me that I didn't even know it myself. There was too much shame going on in the present to even let it leak through. I was ashamed of landing myself in hospital yet again, of the fact that Fintan had hated me so much, of what I had done to my children over the years, of what I was doing to Frank, of what I was doing to my new baby daughter, who Frank was still keeping away from me. But underpinning all this shame was another level of self-hatred that I had not yet connected with.

Although *Sentimental Killer* had been a success, my reputation as a drinker had made me *persona non grata* with the powers-that-be in the Irish music industry. Elvis Costello had been asked to do some songs for a project called *Bringing It All Back Home*, a five-part documentary for RTÉ tracing the history of Irish music from traditional beginnings to the present. A companion CD was being made to go with the series.

'Why haven't you been asked to do it, Mary?' Elvis said when he read the line up, which involved the cream of Irish talent. I shrugged my shoulders and said something about the drink, but he just couldn't understand why I had been left out.

He had been given carte blanche by those calling the shots on *Bringing It All Back Home*, so he suggested to me that I duet with him on a beautiful new song called 'Mischievous Ghost' that he'd written for the project. He asked them for a full orchestra in the studio, which he got, and we recorded it.

At the same time, he gave me a cassette of songs he thought I should record. One of them was a song he had just written called 'Upon a Veil of Midnight Blue'. That song means an awful lot to me still.

Elvis was a director of a small label called Demon Records, and he suggested that they give me a deal to do an album. Erik and I decided to make the album live, to capture my performance. I contacted Vince Power at the Mean Fiddler in London, who gave the idea an immediate thumbs-up.

A live album of new songs was something not often done: live albums are usually made up of an artist's known repertoire. There was a huge amount of preparatory work needed to get the songs right. It was during one of my sober times, when I had just come out of hospital. Vince had the idea that we should do the album over a week of gigs in the Mean Fiddler, with a mobile studio in one of the dressing rooms for Erik to work in. The box office takings from the shows would pay for the recording and mixing.

In the lead-up to and during the week of recording, I stayed with Neil in his flat in St John's Wood. The Oscar nominations were about to be announced and word was that *The Crying Game* would be getting a few nods. The guy who had played the transvestite character in the film, Jay Davidson, was hiding out in the flat because the press were going crazy about whether he would be nominated for Best Supporting Actor or Actress. He was there with his boyfriend from Dublin, who was a hairdresser, and there were big, burly security men outside.

While they were setting the whole recording situation up in the Mean Fiddler, Erik was desperately afraid I would drink and he put a guy from the band, Dick Farrelly, on the lookout. Dick was always going on about how he was an absolute insomniac and never slept a wink. So he was stationed on a mattress outside my bedroom door. At the crack of dawn the day of the first recording session, I opened the door and there was Dick, snoring away, without a care in the world. I tiptoed out, found a bottle of gin in the kitchen and poured myself a glass. I was absolutely trolleyed by the time everyone else woke up.

Erik went ape. 'How dare you!' he screamed at me. 'You're wasting my time, you're wasting the band's time, wasting everyone's time! Go back to bed and fucking get yourself together for tonight.'

Erik went in and told every person working in the Mean Fiddler that I was not to be served any alcohol. He showed me the CCTV cameras outside my dressing room when I got there later that day. 'We're watching you, Mary,' he said.

A man was employed to watch me too. 'If she sneaks out a door or crawls out a window, drag her back,' he was told. Every day while they were doing their sound checks, they locked me in the dressing room. I tried my best to get out, even going so far as to try and remove the bars on the window, but I was caught every time.

Eventually a bargain was struck, whereby if I stayed sober for the next four nights, while they were recording *Love for Sale*, I would be allowed to drink after the last session was done.

The gigs were some of the best I have ever done and the crowd loved the new songs. We all worked really well together in that band. There was Paul Moore on double bass, James Delaney on piano and Hammond organ, Robbie Casserly on drums, Dick Farrelly on guitar and Richie Buckley on the saxophone. There was a lot of intuitive jamming, and it all really came together on stage: we were hot. One time I looked over at James and he was tearing into the Hammond so hard that his fingers were bleeding.

Soon after we were finished recording, the Oscar nominations were announced. Neil had a room at The Groucho Club and the two of us were there, waiting for the news. I felt very special being there, and, of course, when *The Crying Game* was nominated for Best Director and Best Original Screenplay, we all went absolutely bananas. The subsequent bender lasted two days.

Neil was a good friend to me. He stuck with me through thick and thin with the drinking. I puked in a bed in his home one night while he was trying to dry me out, something I will eternally be embarrassed for.

He always had a lot of respect for me, and he'd always come to gigs. One night, in Dublin, he brought Mick Jagger to a gig in Whelan's, but there was no sign of me on stage. The doors were closed, and the owner of the place, Dave Allen, was on the phone with Frank, going: 'Where the fuck is she? The place is jammed, Mick Jagger is here, and we're all fucking waiting.'

I was at home in my room on my mattress, legless. 'I'm finished with this shit,' Frank told Dave. 'I'm not dragging her out anymore.'

On other occasions, when I was too pissed to do a gig, he and Aoife and Ollie would pull me out of the bed, throw me into the shower and keep me under the water until I sobered up. But this time, they let me be. I was banned after that from ever playing in Whelan's again.

*

Two years it lasted. Two miserable, stinking, rotten, bitter, drink-sodden years, during which my children, and Frank, grew to hate me as much as I hated myself. During which my eldest daughter had to move out of home, so she could do her Leaving Certificate. During which I beat her younger sister for pouring a bottle of vodka down the sink.

During one of my stretches of sobriety, I became pregnant again. I knew quickly that I was expecting. Despite the fact that I had killed so many brain cells with alcohol, I was very in touch with the changes in my body that pregnancy instantly brings about. Here, I thought once more, was the answer.

I had never drunk while I was pregnant with any of my other children, and I promised myself that this time would be no different. This pregnancy was the wake-up call I needed, the signal that enough was enough and that I had to get my life back into shape. I poured the last of the vodka in the house and in my hiding places down the drain, straightened myself up, and prepared to bring another child into the world in complete sobriety.

Ten weeks into the pregnancy, Frank came home to find me passed out and paralytic on the kitchen floor, with a piece of bread and butter stuck my hair. He got me up, packed me into the car and brought me to the mental hospital in Newcastle. Nobody else would take me. They must have given me a Xanax or something, because I dozed off into the blackness.

When I woke up, I felt as if I had wet myself. I pulled the covers back, looked down and saw that I was bleeding: big clots of dark, red blood were pooling on the white sheets. I threw myself out of the bed and knelt in the middle of the floor, and started screaming and screaming. There was blood everywhere. My hands were covered in it, I was holding my hair and screaming, and it was running down the side of my head. I was so hysterical that eventually somebody slapped me across the face to shut me up.

They brought me by ambulance to Holles Street hospital. Lying in the cubicle, waiting for the doctor to come and examine me, I was in an agony of guilt. I had damaged my living children, I had damaged myself, and now I had damaged the unborn.

The doctor came in and said: 'We are going to give you a D & C, Mrs Coughlan.'

Big, fat tears rolled down my cheeks as they administered the anaesthetic.

Because my liver, my kidneys and all my organs were in such a state from alcohol poisoning, I developed a condition called metabolic acidosis under the anaesthetic. I was transferred from Holles Street by speeding ambulance to the Mater Hospital. I remember the siren and a mad dash of people around me when we arrived. I was put in the intensive care ward.

A doctor said to me: 'Mary. I'm going to have to cut your throat, just along here,' and he mimed where the incision would be on his own throat. 'I have to do it so I can put tubes in and get some medication to your heart, but there'll be no scar, okay?'

I nodded, yes.

About five years later, I was signing CDs after a show at the jazz festival in Cork, when a man held his CD out for me to autograph. 'Mary,' he says, 'I'm going to have to cut your throat, just along here.' I looked up and saw the doctor who had saved my life. 'Do you remember those words?' he asked. 'Do I?' I replied. 'I'll never fucking forget them!'

I was given hours to live. 'We should send for her family,' one of the doctors said. 'Is there anybody we should call?' he asked. I shook my head, no.

Frank arrived. 'What have you done now?' he asked, when he saw the state of me. I couldn't speak: I had an oxygen mask on and tubes sticking out of my throat. He told me he never wanted to see me again, and then he walked out.

The doctors had to ascertain what condition my liver was in, and all my other organs. So they injected me with radioactive stuff and put me in isolation. When the nurses came in, they had to put on lead aprons because I was radioactive.

It was touch-and-go, but, like my grandmother in Donegal, I am as strong as a horse. I made a miraculous recovery and a couple of days later, I found myself back on a normal ward, sitting up in bed. The kids came in to visit, but only to tell me that they hated me and that they didn't want me home.

The newspapers reported what had happened. 'Mary Coughlan has been hospitalised, having suffered serious complications after a miscarriage.' The room began to fill up with flowers.

I was very grateful at the time that I was spared the full glare of the media spotlight, which could have revealed far more than just the surface detail. If it had happened today, the story would have been plastered all over the tabloids, and my family would have suffered hugely. But I knew an awful lot of the journalists from my days drinking in Mulligans with Frank Miller, and they stayed away. They didn't intrude.

It was St Patrick's weekend, and I was aware that outside everyone was drinking and having a great old time. The only person I felt safe calling was a woman from the AA fellowship who had taken a keen interest in me since we met in St John of God. She was sober and wanted to help me get sober too. 'What am I going to do?' I asked her. 'How am I going to stop myself from drinking, if I don't even know why I'm doing it?'

She said: 'You've got to help yourself, Mary. I've spoken with Frank and the kids, and they don't want you to go back home. You should stay with me when you're discharged from here.'

I was ten days in the Mater, worrying about the poor baby that had lost its life, and why my tortured body had been chosen for him to come into the world. Maybe he was just another tortured soul who didn't want to be reincarnated and chose me, knowing full well that I would push him out of my body with alcohol.

It was decided that I would go to the Rutland Centre, a private alcohol and drug rehabilitation centre in Dublin that had the reputation of getting the worst junkies, gamblers, alcoholics and other addicts to face up to their addictions. It was seen in Ireland at the time as the absolute end of the line.

I was booked to go in at the end of March, but we had no money to pay for it. I called Vince Power and asked him for help. Without blinking an eye, he said: 'How much do you need?' He sent it over the next day.

When I got out of the Mater, there were two gigs that I was still lined up to do. Frank said: 'We'll let you home if you do the two gigs.'

So, even though I was barely able to stand up, I did them and earned enough money to pay the mortgage for the time I would be away in rehab. At least I was good for something.

When I was drinking and being admitted to hospitals over and over again, Frank would say to me: 'Do you think, Mary, that this is the last time you're going to do this? Because I can't put up with much more, and neither can the kids.'

I'd say: 'I don't know.'

'What the fuck do you mean, you don't know?' he'd shout. 'Just make up your fucking mind.' But I couldn't do that. I couldn't make up my mind.

As I packed my bag for the Rutland Centre, he asked me the same thing. 'This is the last time,' I said.

I was lower than lino. I had reached my rock bottom: there was no further down for me to go. The Rutland Centre was my last hope.

16

'I Can't Make You Love Me'

Every Tuesday in the Rutland Centre was 'Family Day'. When you went in there first, it was legend among the other 'clients', as the Centre like to call us. Those who had been through Family Day, those who were about to face it: everyone talked about it in hushed, terrified tones.

Family Day was reality therapy. No mercy was spared, as the members of your family confronted you about what you had done and how it had left them feeling.

On Family Day number one, I couldn't look at the kids. I sat there and listened to them and Frank giving out about me. Giving out, and giving out, and giving out. I wasn't allowed to open my mouth to retaliate or make excuses: answering back was against the rules.

We weren't alone. There were a few families in the room, all in a circle, with two counsellors to facilitate the confrontations. There would be spouses, children, mothers, fathers, even grandparents there, and each would be invited to speak to the addict in their family. So, not only did my family get to confront me about how I had hurt them, they got to listen to other families and realise that they were not alone in their hurt. The experiences of the children and partners, parents and grandparents of addicts may differ in the detail, but in matters of the heart, they are essentially the same.

Before they were to go into the Family Day session, the family members were encouraged by counsellors, and given, for example, helpful strategies around handling fear. They were told to take an incident and to speak about it, if they felt they could. There was no pressure.

During the session, there was no place for me to hide. You couldn't hide from the fellow 'inmates' in your group, you couldn't hide from their families, you couldn't hide from your own family, and you certainly couldn't hide from yourself.

Aoife talked about listening to me throw up all night long, and worrying that I would choke on my vomit and die. About having to move out of home at the age of seventeen, so that she could do her exams. Ollie talked about witnessing my head being put through a wall by the boyfriend who nearly destroyed our lives, and the time I hit her for pouring my vodka down the sink. Frank talked about what it was like to be left holding a six-week-old baby, trying to feed her baby formula with a dropper and a spoon, because I could no longer breastfeed her. Aoife and Ollie talked about trying to hold me up when I was drunk, about trying to get my nipple into baby Clare's mouth when she was roaring with hunger.

I listened and I listened. Week after week, I heard what they were saying to me. I felt guilty, I felt ashamed, I felt disgusted with myself, but something about what they were saying wasn't getting through. A part of me was cut off from their complaints, from their anger and their grief. A part of me felt so overwhelmingly sorry for myself, that I couldn't properly feel sorry for them, or for what I had put them through.

Then one day, my little Eoin spoke up. At the time I was in the Rutland, he was twelve going on thirteen, and he spoke of the time we lived in Howth when he was a much younger child.

He talked of how I would go to the pub with my friend, bringing Eoin along, and how I would buy him a Coke and a bag of crisps and send him off into a corner while I drank for hours. It was like it happened every day, as far as he was concerned. 'I was lonely,' he said. 'I thought you didn't want me around.'

It was such a simple and true thing. My little boy, alone and unwanted. More than all the horrors of drinking four bottles of vodka a day in front of my children, or bringing abusive men into their lives, this little kernel of truth hit me like a ton of bricks. That night I cried and cried in my bed. My heart was not broken for myself, it was broken for my children. For my lonely, motherless children. For the first time I began to realise what it was like for other people when I was drinking.

The next morning, we got up at seven a.m. as usual to do our chores. We had to clean the toilets, get the breakfast and clean up afterwards. And then I went to visit my counsellor, a woman called Yvonne.

'How are you today, Mary?' she asked.

'Oh, grand,' I said.

'What do you mean, you're grand? I was there yesterday, listening to your kids. They're amongst the most hurt children I ever met.'

I had had a revelation about the truth from Eoin, but I had snapped back into the pretence that everything was A-OK, that there was nothing wrong with Mary, nothing she couldn't handle.

That is what the Rutland Centre experience was like. It was a relentless process of forward steps and backward steps, revelations turning to self-delusion, before the confrontations would start all over again and you'd be pitched into a deep well of self-pity.

But at the end, it began to dawn on me that alcoholism, like other addictions, is a hereditary disease. There was absolutely nothing you could do about it, except not drink. Not take heroin. Not gamble. Not overeat. Not starve yourself.

I also began to learn the ways in which my family unit had become emotionally dependent on my drinking. When you're an alcoholic, the people around you and living with you have a vested interest in keeping you drunk. It part of what's known as codependency. Your drunkenness justifies the way that they feel about life. The family has one big scapegoat in the alcoholic, and they focus all the blame in that direction, never getting to fully look at or take responsibility for themselves.

Everything is the alcoholic's fault, so in a way it suits everyone if the alcoholic is drinking, or falls off the wagon. At the end of my time drinking, Frank was buying me vodka. He was contributing to me being the way I was and that gave him the excuse to continue keeping Clare away from me. I was in no fit condition to be her mother, and as long as I was drinking, this would continue to be the case.

If the alcoholic stops drinking, the feelings that once had

such rightful justification don't just go away. It's the next step – how the family and the alcoholic deal with the absence of justification – that matters hugely in the healing process. As my time came to an end in the Rutland Centre, I was fully aware of this. It was going to take a very, very long time for them to be able to trust me: it wasn't going to happen immediately.

While I was going through all this, a call came from the people organising a follow-up to the hugely successful *A Woman's Heart* album and tour, but I had decided that I'd had enough of the music industry. For all the joy I got out of singing and recording, it was just too dangerous a place for a recovering alcoholic. Yet at the same time, I was yearning to sing again.

'It's not for another six months,' my counsellor said, when I told her about my confusion. 'Singing is an enormous part of who you are, Mary. Letting go of it won't bring you peace of mind or happiness: it will bring the opposite. Say yes to the concerts and use the time between then and now to prepare yourself to do them in good health.'

I got out the day after my thirty-eighth birthday, on 6 May. Once I was home, all I had to do was to not drink. Help was available through AA, and a counsellor was going to be there for me at the Rutland Centre, every Tuesday for the next two years. These were the only commitments I had to make in life: not to drink, and to go to my counselling sessions.

I went home, drove to the off-licence, bought a bottle of vodka and got slaughtered.

When I'd drained the bottle, I called the Rutland. They told me to go to bed and come in the next day to see a counsellor.

The woman they assigned to my case was called Maura Russell. When I went in that afternoon, she sat me down and said, 'You're not going to have any chance at all unless you stop fooling yourself. You need to tell me what exactly is going on for you.'

I knew that to have a shot at real recovery, I had to tell one other human being what was in my heart. And Maura was that person.

And out it all it came. All about the abuse, all about my father and my feelings towards my mother. It wasn't in the one session. Maura was my counsellor for many years, and I learned to trust her in a way I had never trusted anyone ever before. She never judged me. In her presence, all the things that had been in my head, my heart and my soul since the age of four came out.

Once a week, for two years, I went to see Maura. I spoke to her about the deepest, darkest feelings I had about Frank. I spoke to her about my separation from Clare, about the baby I believed I had killed, about everything that was going on inside me.

One afternoon, I watched a movie on television about a woman who was dying of cancer. This woman's family looked after her. At the end, after she came home from the hospital for the last time, they took her bed down into the living room and had all these deep, meaningful conversations with her, telling her they loved her.

I cried so much, I thought there would be no end to my tears. As the credits rolled, I was so distraught I rang Maura. 'I would never want to look after my mother if she was sick. I would never do that,' I sobbed down the phone.

Maura replied: 'The right of every child is to have the love, protection and affection of their parents. It was your right to be loved, to feel safe and to love in return.'

I had always felt there was something missing in my Ma. She took care of us in all sorts of ways – making clothes, cooking, washing, ironing – but she was emotionally absent. I had become the same way with my own children.

'We have some very important work to do, Mary,' Maura said. 'You have to go back to the very core of your pain. You have to take the hurt little girl inside you by the hand and tell her it's OK now, nothing bad is going to happen again, it's all over.'

And so we began the sessions where I would become a little girl once more, a little girl who was being abused. I had to go through every bit of it again. I went back to places of abject terror and absolute helplessness. I took that little girl by the hand and whispered to her that it was not her fault. She did not invite sexual abuse; she did not make it happen. I reassured her again and again, hoping she would hear me, that she would finally get the message.

I began to find out that I had in some way remained a four-year-old all my life: a sexually abused, physically and emotionally violated child. All my life, that's the place I had gone back to every single time anybody hurt me. It was affirmed to me, every day, that I was not a good person. Whether it was at school or whether it was fighting with my sisters at home and getting clattered for it. Whether it was leaving Fintan, or leaving my children behind while I got on with my career. Whether it was losing everything because I signed away my house, or throwing myself down the bottom of a bottle. I was forever a little girl who was rotten to the core, who deserved the bad things life threw at her, who didn't deserve anything good.

During the time I was drinking, there were a few occasions when I had what I now understand were flashbacks, the same kind of experience as that first time I went on stage and nothing came out of my mouth: that feeling of being made of wafer-thin ice.

I remember standing at the kitchen sink one morning, peeling potatoes, when this terror came over me. Everything became icy and I could see myself standing there, with the whole world stopped dead around me. Now I know that I was going back to that place, to the moments when I was being sexually abused and my spirit was being exposed to pain and fear on a very deep level. 'Here it comes,' I would say to myself, and I'd go running to the nearest pub or off-licence to separate myself from the horror of it all with alcohol.

Along with my one-to-one sessions with Maura, I would go to group therapy every Tuesday night at the Rutland. You were supposed to be with your partner, or a child, or somebody in your family. Although he didn't like it, Frank came along for the most part of two years.

Through this process, it became more and more apparent that Frank still harboured terrible anger towards me. During the group sessions, I took all the blame for everything that happened, while Frank went on about all the terrible things I did. The more he said, the more I wallowed in guilt.

One night, I was wallowing away when the group facilitator, a guy called Declan, said: 'Get off the fucking cross, Mary.'

He turned to Frank and said: 'It's been two years since Mary drank. Now, are you in this relationship with her or not?'

It became very clear to me that he wasn't.

Frank would never let me get Clare dressed in the morning, he would never allow me to even change her nappy. She was his child and I didn't deserve her.

They had a hole in her bedroom floor where he used to hide sweets for her. One day she held her finger up to her mouth and said: 'Shhh. Don't tell Mammy,' and showed me the hiding place.

I told myself to accept the fact that Frank was never going to trust me again. I had hurt him so badly and he'd had to put up with so much, I had no right to expect his forgiveness. 'Shut the fuck up, and grin and bear it, bitch,' I said to myself. 'You're alive, you've got a family, you're not drinking and you're getting better.'

The first year after I stopped drinking, I hated every bastard that drank. Neil and his girlfriend, Brenda, would come over every single Sunday for dinner. Frank would cook his famous meatballs with spaghetti, and afterwards they'd leave me with all the kids and head off to the Harbour Bar. I hated them all.

During the drinking, I had several places that I would go to and drink secretly in the car. Bullock Harbour in Dalkey was one of them. I'd pull up there and drink a naggin of vodka. One day, about twelve months after I came out of the Rutland, I drove to Bullock Harbour to see what it was like. I think I was testing myself.

The still, icy feeling came over me. It felt like the car filled up with alcohol. I could taste it on my tongue: Gordon's gin and tonic, with a slice of lemon.

I pulled out my phone and rang Maura.

'How do you feel?' she asked.

'I feel great,' I said. 'I've never been closer to me. I don't want the drink. I want this, what I have now.'

And then I asked her: 'Is it all right to say that I'm never going to drink again?'

She said: 'If you want to say that, you can.'

I said: 'Maura, I am never going to drink again.'

Doing *A Woman's Heart II* was a way of dipping my big toe into it all again, without having to take on a whole tour of my own, or doing my own gigs. They asked me to record a new track for the album, and the song I chose was 'I Can't Make You Love Me', which was a perfect expression of where I was with Frank.

They also included 'Invisible to You' from *Uncertain Pleasures* on the album and I did a short tour, back in the company of Mary Black, along with her sister, Frances, Sharon Shannon and Maura O'Connell.

I was singing better than ever, and the concerts boosted my confidence a little. I decided I would like to try out a few new gigs of my own. I knew I didn't want to go the big route any more. I wasn't getting a manager; I wasn't getting an agent. I would put my own three-piece band together and I would ring up all the places that I'd played in before to ask them for work. I started with John Mannion, the owner of the Róisín Dubh in Galway.

'Fuck off, Mary,' John said in no uncertain terms. 'You fell off the stage the last time you were here.'

I swore that I wasn't drinking anymore, that I'd do the gig as sober as the soberest judge. 'I'm not giving you any money,' said John. 'We'll do a small gig during the Arts Festival and I won't pay you until you're finished.'

He rang me back the following week and said: 'All the tickets are gone. Will you do another night?'

'Okay,' I said.

A few days later, he rang back again and said: 'Can you do five nights? Can you do six? What about eight, with a matinee?'

It was my return to Galway, and I was more nervous than I had been about any other gig I had ever done. I know there is a video in existence of my last terrible, drunken performance there, something I never want to watch as long as I live. Hopefully it will never find its way on to YouTube.

I rang Erik and told him I was doing the Róisín Dubh, and he got very excited. 'Let's record it,' he said. '"Mary Coughlan Live in Galway!"'

I sang my heart out for a week, renting a house and bringing all the family down. Eoin was there with his pals and he came to the gigs with Aoife and Ollie. My mother was there every night and people I had been at school with. People I hung out with in the hippie days actually paid to get in. It was amazing.

The last song of the set was a cover of Sam Cooke's 'You Send Me'. The audience went wild for it, stomping their feet and whooping. When I sang it on my final night in the Róisín Dubh, I was so completely overcome with what I can only describe as love, I made a speech afterwards. I have no idea what I said, but I was crying tears of joy. Everyone stood up and, I swear to Jesus, they clapped for ten minutes. I felt that after years in the wilderness, I had finally made it home.

For the next two years, *Live in Galway* was my life and livelihood. I toured everywhere with my little band, made up of Brian Connor, Kieran Wilde and Conor Barry. We could all fit in one car, so it made the whole thing easier and the CDs sold like hotcakes after each gig. I actually felt like I was in control of my life, for the first time ever. I was the one calling the shots with my career and drink wasn't dragging me into the gutter.

Neil began working on the *Michael Collins* movie in Dublin. He asked me to work with Julia Roberts, who was preparing to sing 'She Moved Through the Fair' in the film, playing Kitty Kiernan opposite Liam Neeson as Collins and Aidan Quinn as Harry Boland.

I had spoken to Julia when I was doing *High Spirits*, but now that she was a big star, I was sick with nerves at the thought of meeting her. I tried on everything I had in the house and when I couldn't find anything, I went into A-Wear and bought a white blouse and a black skirt, and a black linen jacket – clothes I would never have normally worn – to try and make an impression.

Julia turned up to meet me in an old pair of jeans and a T-shirt, looking like a million dollars. She had CDs of mine, which she had been listening to for my accent and singing along with. She loved 'Ancient Rain', she told me while we were working on 'She Moved Through the Fair' in Waltons School of Music.

She would listen to my voice as I was talking and the way I sang. We went on a stroll through St Stephen's Green, and at one point she started saying: 'Imagine, Yeats walked here,' or,

'Imagine, James Joyce might have sat on this very bench with his Nora.'

We sat down and she took a piece of board on to which were painted the black and white keys of a piano. She had to be playing the piano in the film and she didn't know how to, so she wanted her fingering to look perfect. Every time we sat down somewhere, she'd take out that little piece of board and start tapping away on it.

At home, Frank became more and more focused on Clare. Nobody was ever going to hurt Clare like I had hurt her and abandoned her. He said this to me on a daily basis.

He couldn't forgive me for losing the other baby. I knew that it was a little boy that I lost, because Frank had asked them to do a postmortem. I asked him to come to my sessions with Maura to confront his anger, and he came to a couple. He told her he wasn't angry. That he had put it behind him.

But he was angry. I felt it every day. It was a constant anger that underpinned life in our house. After a while, I decided to be as good to Frank as I could possibly be. Every day, I said to myself, be kind to him, forget the anger, just focus on the positive. I wanted to help him get over it at his own pace.

I dreamed one night that I had a beautiful, brown-eyed baby boy, and when I woke up I knew that I wanted another child. I didn't know how I was going to do it, because Frank and I weren't having anything like a sexual relationship.

For Valentine's Day, I booked a night away for us in Tinakilly House. I told Frank we were just going to dinner, and he was anxious enough about leaving Clare with Aoife and Ollie for just that. The girls were all excited for me as I packed an overnight bag with a new blue silk nightie, and hid it in the back of the car. I was forty, my biological clock was ticking like a time bomb, and I was a woman on a mission. I wanted to get pregnant.

When we got there, I took the bag out of the back and said: 'Surprise! We're staying the night.'

'No way,' he said. 'I'm not staying here: I have to go home to Clare.'

'She's fucking four years of age, Frank,' I said. 'She's happy with Aoife and Ollie minding her.'

I begged him to come into the hotel. 'Just stay for dinner. If you really want to go after that, okay,' I said. 'We need this time alone.'

Eventually, he gave in and we checked into the room. That evening we had a lovely romantic dinner, Frank drank a bottle of wine, and we went up to our four-poster bed.

When I woke up the next morning, I was pregnant.

17

'After the Fall'

I knew I was pregnant very quickly, and in my bones I knew that I was going to have a boy. Happy and contented, I got back to my regular life, touring with my little band, doing gigs across Ireland and Europe, selling the *Live in Galway* CD afterwards. Vince invited us to play the Mean Fiddler again: the first time I'd been back there since recording *Love for Sale*. I was in the dressing room after the show when a man popped his head around the door and said: 'Hi, can I talk to you for a minute?'

His name was Steve Abbot, and he was setting up a new record label for Richard Branson, called V2 Records. It was a subsidiary of Virgin Records, featuring different kinds of acts to the main label. I was the first one they were approaching to be signed.

'We want to buy the rights to your *Live in Galway* CD and put it out as a taster for a new album we'd like you to record,' Steve said.

'Here we go again,' I thought. A big record deal with

Richard Branson; the whole show back on the road again, with everything that entailed. But I wasn't scared any more. I'd been sober for three years now and I was determined to enjoy life and live every minute to the full.

The new album was to be released on the Big Cat label for V2. Steve had owned Big Cat as a small indie label. Now that Richard Branson had bought it over, Steve had just hit the big time.

Before recording began, six months later, I was asked to give a series of intimate promotional concerts in Belgium, Holland and Germany to promote *Live in Galway* and get the industry talking about me again. Although I was pregnant and easily tired, I was up for it nonetheless.

Our tour manager had gotten a chip van from his friend and converted it into a bus, complete with hard wooden benches screwed to the floor in the back and a sliding door on the passenger's side. Seatbelts were not a priority. Halfway from Holland to Germany, as we were speeding down the autobahn, the sliding door fell off and went flying into the hard shoulder, the wind nearly sucking us all out of the van along with it.

We pulled the van in, gaffer-taped the door back on and then exited for the nearest town, where Erik came to meet us. When he saw the van, Erik rang Steve in England.

'This is lunacy!' he shouted. 'You have a pregnant woman who shouldn't be doing these gigs anyway, and you have her touring around Europe sitting on a bench in a chip van with a door taped to its side?'

He told us to park the van at the station and get a train to where we were going. We threw the keys under the mat, and left the van there, the tour manager grumbling about having to spend money on our train tickets.

Alarm bells should have gone off, but they didn't even sound somewhere in the distance. I was delighted to be back on the road, singing better than ever and not drinking.

After the Fall was an album about recovery. Ten years earlier, I had heard Jimmy McCarthy singing a number called 'I'm Still in Love' in Slattery's pub on Dublin's Capel Street, but it was an unfinished song. During my time in the Rutland Centre, I wrote hundreds of verses to that song. Everything was four lines long, ending with the refrain, 'I'm Still in Love'. It was the perfect song about optimism in the face of a thousand defeats, so when I started casting around for numbers to include on *After the Fall*, I asked Jimmy if I could I could finish the song, which he agreed to. I hadn't written my own songs before, so this was a perfect way to begin. I also wrote a song called 'Run Away Teddy' with Johnny Mulhern, which was about the night I went over to kill my ex-boyfriend at his house on the South Circular Road.

The last track on the album was an old Purcell piece called 'When I Am Laid in Earth (Dido's Lament)', a song about asking for forgiveness. I did a few takes, but Erik kept saying it wasn't faithful to the original version.

'You're not singing it properly,' he said over and over again.

'Well, it's the only way I know how to do it,' I shot back. 'I'm not a fucking opera singer.'

'You're not even singing the right notes,' Erik replied. 'It's a classical piece, it's one of the most beautiful pieces ever written, and you're ruining it.'

I wanted to record an a cappella version of it. 'Can I not just do it like I did "Strange Fruit?"' I asked. 'It hadn't the exact notes either, but that version of it became mine.'

Erik called my piano player, Brian Connor, and said: 'Will you come in and listen to how Mary is destroying this song?'

Connor thought my version was beautiful and told Erik so.

'If you sing it like that, I'm taking my name off the production credits for that song,' Erik snapped, and I replied: 'Take your fucking name off it, I don't care. I'm going to sing it the way I want to sing it.'

It was the first time I'd ever spoken to Erik like that. It was the first time I had challenged him and was comfortable enough in myself to do it. The ensuing fight was nasty, and before he went back to Holland, he said to Frank: 'She would be nothing if it wasn't for me.'

Like everyone else, Erik was used to me being out of control and to doing everything for me. We had a rare and brilliant creative partnership, but now he needed to recognise it as a partnership of equals. He had said to me at one stage during the recording: 'You're different now – I don't know what to do.'

While we were recording *After the Fall*, the National Irish Bank continued to pursue me for the money I owed them. When they had taken the money from the sale of my house in Howth, I still owed them £20,000, and in the intervening years that had become about £27,000 worth of debt. They brought criminal proceedings against me in the High Court.

'Mary, we're really sorry, but we have a warrant to take you into custody,' a Garda said, arriving at Martello Terrace with a paddywagon.

I stuck my belly out as far as I could and said: 'But you can't do that to me, I'm pregnant.'

Inside I was thinking: 'Bring it on. It will look great for the National Irish Bank in the newspapers: "Heavily pregnant Mary Coughlan carted off to prison for non-payment of debt".'

'Is there nothing you can do?" the Garda said. He was very reluctant to arrest me.

I rang Steve Abbot, and told him what was happening. 'Tell them to give you a few days, Mary,' he said. 'I'm going to call Branson.'

V2 did a deal with the bank. They reduced my debt significantly; he made an immediate payment on my behalf, which was my advance for *After the Fall*.

I went into labour at the party in Dublin Castle following the premiere of *Michael Collins*. Natasha Richardson and Nora Owen were with me in the bathroom when the first pains came. 'You'll have to call it Michael if it's a boy,' Nora (a grand-niece of Collins) said.

'I might call it Aidan, after Aidan Quinn,' I laughed. The night had been spent marvelling at Quinn's gorgeous blue eyes.

In the end I called my brown-eyed boy Cian, which means 'ancient warrior'. He was born on 7 November 1997 in Holles Street hospital, and he was exactly as I dreamed he would be.

This time, there was no reason for Frank to take my baby away from me. From the moment he came into the world, Cian was my little companion.

When he was seven days old, the two of us travelled to the North, so that I could appear in a Brian Kennedy Special at the university at Coleraine, which was being filmed for television by UTV. Before I left, I went out and bought a hideous blue velvet Laura Ashley trouser suit, which, in my post-delivery, hormonal state, I had thought was only gorgeous. I was as fat as a queen bee and at least the suit actually fitted, which was a start. Seeing myself on television later made me laugh out loud: my tits looked like a pair of giant watermelons stuffed into a blue velvet blanket.

Van Morrison was possibly going to turn up for the show, but there was no sign of him and, in a bit of a panic at the very last minute, Brian said: 'Will you sing Van's song with me? Do you know the words of "Crazy Love"?'

'I think I do,' I said and the two of us walked onto the stage.

When the band started up, I couldn't remember the words. I was mumbling bits and singing the lines I knew by heart from listening to the album years ago, with Brian looking over at me in bewilderment. But in the end we got through it.

After that, I went to London with Cian to do some early promo interviews for *After the Fall*, which was due out in February 1997. I didn't want to stay in the Columbia Hotel, because I associated it with the heavy drinking days of *High Spirits* and the *Under the Influence* tour, so I asked V2 to book me into another place. They got me a room in a low-rent hotel, which was a hideous knocking shop with stained net curtains.

Rooms could be rented by the hour and all sorts of shady types were coming and going, day and night.

Alone in my room with the baby, I was terrified. The thought occurred to me that I could have a drink and nobody would be the wiser. There was an off-licence next door.

'Just the one,' I told myself. 'It will do no harm.' But then I realised that it could never be just the one. All the work I had put in so far would be flushed down the toilet if I took that drink. So, I bundled the baby up and walked up Queensway in the freezing cold to the Columbia Hotel, to show Cian off to the staff. Then I was sorry I didn't stay there. They were all around me, delighted with my new baby, treating me like one of the family.

When I got back to the knocking shop, I put the chest of drawers up against the door and tried to get some sleep, alcohol-free.

For all my leaps forward, it was becoming increasingly difficult for Frank to deal with the sober Mary. Like most people in this world, he had his own history to deal with, his own baggage.

'That's why we were attracted to each other in the first place,' I told him. 'Even though we are very different people on the outside, on the inside we are a pair of really small, damaged, lonely kids.'

When I left the Rutland, we had jointly embarked on a two-year after-care programme, but Frank had not completed it with me. I gave him an ultimatum: 'Get yourself some therapy or we're never going to be happy together.' So Frank went back to after-care at the Rutland Centre.

When *After the Fall* was released, it got a *Rolling Stone* Critic's Choice award, and was named one of the best albums of 1997 in *Billboard* magazine. The album was to be my introduction to the American market: it was to make my name there. But first there were some European dates to do.

As I was due to fly off to do the first *After the Fall* concert in Holland, Frank insisted that I leave Cian at home. I couldn't sleep the night before I left. I had terrible dreams and woke up in a panic, thinking: 'If I go on the plane, it's going to crash and I'll never see Cian again.'

I told Frank about my dream, and he said: 'If any plane's going to crash, you're going to go down on your own. I'm keeping the child and that's that.'

I went alone and did the gig and it was fine. But that night, after I had finished singing, I started longing for something. Something to kill the pain of what was going on at home with Frank, the pain of not being able to get over the guilt, of not being allowed to get over what I had done to him. I walked up to somebody and asked if there would be any chance of getting some cocaine. Thankfully, there wasn't.

I kept Cian with me after that. By this stage, Aoife was twenty and Ollie was eighteen, so they took it in turns to come with me and mind him while I was singing. 'I'd Rather Go Blind' was the final number of the set, and whenever I started singing it, I'd hear Cian start crying in the dressing room. He knew it was the last song and that any moment now he was going to get fed. We travelled the length and breadth of England and Europe and then went to America, where the plan was to get me as much exposure as possible.

Dan Beck was the managing director of V2 there, and he took me, Cian and Ollie out to dinner. 'This is gonna be huge,' he said, and we toasted with a glass of water.

It was my first time in America. I was on the cover of *The Music Magazine* and everyone was going crazy, but there was nothing really going on to back it up. There were no wheels in motion to capitalise on any momentum that had been built. Dan was a true professional and he was pushing, but he could only do so much. There were hundreds of other people working in the company, doing nothing for the album. America is a huge country and to break it, you have to be as organised as a SWAT team.

I worked my arse off. With my baby in my arms, I traipsed across the States, coast to coast. From New York to Baltimore, Washington up to Detroit, Chicago, Boston, Philadelphia, all the way over to the other side of the country, and in between. It was really tough, but we were getting good audiences. I did twenty-minute gigs in the afternoons in all the Borders bookstores, where the album was being sold. We did TV, radio and press interviews, and for a while it looked as if the album was going to break through.

Cian took his first steps in Chicago. Michael Buckley was getting his saxophone out of its case to do the soundcheck, and Cian pulled himself up and toddled over to him. We all gave him a round of applause, which he accepted graciously, like a chip off the old block.

The boys in the band would come to my room every day and say: 'Can we take the babe magnet out to the park for a walk?'

Three guys out strolling with a gorgeous-looking baby in a

buggy: when girls stopped to admire the kid, they'd be like: 'Oh, yeah, this is our singer's baby – we're giving her a break this afternoon.' In other words, 'It's not our baby, we're available, and we're really lovely, sensitive guys.' They'd invite the women to the gig and sometimes they'd get lucky.

I got a lot of attention in America. Big Cat/V2 were very happy with record sales. I spent the next year and a bit doing gigs on the back of *After the Fall*, mostly in England, sometimes in other parts of Europe, always bringing Cian with me.

To capitalise on the exposure I had had in the States, it was decided that I would quickly record a new album, which would be called *The Long Honeymoon*. V2 in America drafted in Greg Cohen, who had worked with Tom Waits, to produce. I wrote to Erik to tell him. I wanted him to be excited for me to be working with a man who had not only produced Tom Waits, but had played bass in his band for many years, but there was no reply. Erik still had the hump.

I had always wanted to sing 'It Never Entered My Mind', a Rodgers and Hart jazz standard that Peggy Lee had made her own, but over the years, Erik kept refusing to produce it. 'It's just not you,' he'd say. Greg Cohen was a fan of the song, and agreed that it was good for me. It turned out to be one of the most beautiful songs on *The Long Honeymoon* album, and it's a track that still breaks my heart whenever I hear it.

I was very excited to be working alongside Greg, who was unlike any other producer I had ever recorded with. He came to Ireland and personally chose the musicians who would play on the album. One of them was a man called Peter O'Brien, who Greg said was the best pianist in Ireland. An old jazz head, Peter was a bit of a character and well known on the Dublin music scene: he'd accompanied Agnes Bernelle for years. I was delighted to be working with him.

Drummer Wayne Sheehy arrived at the studio with a full set of drums, but was told by Greg to go off and get an oil drum, a baseball bat, sandpaper and a few blocks of wood instead. His entire kit came from a hardware shop! Justin Carroll played harmonium, and my guitarist, Conor Brady, was told to bring along to the studio every stringed instrument he could lay his hands on.

Nancy Sinatra's 'These Boots Are Made for Walking' had been another long-time favourite of mine. I had done a version of it on the *Love for Sale* album, and since then had regularly used it as an encore song at shows. Greg wanted me to do another version of it, and for it he had Conor play an African instrument called a kora. It gave the song a lovely new twist.

The album was recorded in Dublin, but Greg wanted to do the final mixing in New York. While we were there, it became apparent that money wasn't coming through to pay people. We were working on adding a horn section to the album when Greg took me aside and said: 'I hate to bother you with this, Mary, but I haven't been paid any money yet. I need an advance, I have to pay the horn section, I have to pay rental at the studio.'

I called Steve Abbot and he said: 'Don't worry Mary, it's going to be fine. We're just having a few little problems, but they'll be sorted out before you know it.'

Worrying about whether anyone would get paid or not, I took to doing a little recreational cocaine every now and then in the evenings after recording, when we all went out: just a little line here and there. I told myself I was fully in control. Cocaine was not alcohol, and I was an alcoholic, not a drug addict.

We finished working on the album, shot the cover, and I went back to Ireland. A week later, I got the news that Greg would not release the master tapes. He still hadn't been paid. He was right to hold them for ransom: I would have done the same in his shoes. Eventually Big Cat/V2 gave him what he was owed, but still there was no word of releasing the album, no promotion and no interviews.

I was a great one for faxing in those days, before we had e-mail. 'What the fuck is going on?' I faxed Steve. 'You stayed in my house and you've been my friend. Just tell me what's going on.'

Eventually he called me and said: 'We're finished, Mary. It's all gone pear-shaped. I'm going to do everything I can for you to get your CD back.'

I didn't get the master tapes for *Live in Galway* or *After the Fall* back from Big Cat/V2 for another two-and-half years, and only after a series of legal battles. In the meantime, my career, yet again, was up shit creek without a paddle.

The coke – which had begun in New York as a very occasional thing – started infiltrating my life in Dublin. I met someone I'd known years earlier, who was an easy touch for a few lines here and there and, suddenly, every weekend, I was doing lines.

Frank was doing really well. He had set up his own company and patented a thing called the Omniport. He was making plenty of money, swanning off to awards ceremonies with Neil and living the high life. I was back where I felt he wanted me. Forty-four years old and past it, with a cocaine habit and no record deal. A woman who couldn't take care of herself.

18

'All of Me'

My use of cocaine – like my indulgence in every other distraction I had found over the years, from macrobiotics to drinking – began to escalate. And all the while, my relationship with Frank was steadily deteriorating.

Nobody knew about the coke, apart from Frank. I felt that he preferred 'Bad Mary', the one who made him feel like he was in control.

There was no falling down drunk at gigs and I never, ever took the stuff in public. The general perception was that I was as clean as a whistle, the reformed Mary Coughlan with her life back on track, even if there hadn't been an album in a couple of years. And at the time, I really did kid myself that I was sober. I believed my own hype.

The only people who didn't believe the hype were my family. Frank got the children together and told them I was doing coke. 'I'm worried about your mother,' he said.

When I walked into the kitchen that day and found Aoife,

Ollie and Eoin all waiting for me with grim expressions on their faces, I knew the game was up.

'We know you've been doing coke,' Ollie said, with disgust in her eyes.

'Why Mam?' Eoin asked, more hurt than angry. 'You were doing so well.'

From the Family Days during my time at the Rutland, I knew better than to deny, or to answer back. I stood there with my head down, feeling no better than a piece of shit on someone's heel.

'Frank has called the Rutland Centre,' Aoife said. 'You'll have to go back.'

Maura Russell never even batted an eyelid. The kids thought she was going to slap me around the place, and whether she was angry at me, I do not know. It didn't appear so: she gave only unconditional love, acceptance and understanding. I think this made the kids a bit angry, and Frank too: the fact that I didn't get my just punishment for letting them all down.

'You know what you're doing, don't you?' Maura said, when I admitted to her the extent of the problem. 'You're medicating yourself because you are not happy in your life. When are you going to sort out the one thing that's making you unhappy?'

We both knew it was my relationship with Frank: I had said as much in so many sessions. 'You can't deal with it now, though,' Maura said. 'You just have to stop taking the drugs, and deal with things one day at a time for the moment.'

I went back to an after-care programme, every Tuesday night for the best part of a year, taking the same route I had when I was coming off the alcohol, by working on myself, slowly but surely.

At least this time around, there weren't any terrible money worries. Frank's business had really taken off.

In the midst of all this, I got a call from Peter O'Brien, who had played piano on *The Long Honeymoon*. He was doing a series of gigs with different singers in Whelan's.

'Will you come into Whelan's and do a song or two with me?' Peter asked.

'I can't,' I replied. 'I'm fucking barred from Whelan's.'

'I'm sure something like that has never stopped you before,' Peter said, a smile in his voice.

So, I snuck into Whelan's wearing a hoodie, and went up on stage. Driving into town, I had had this voice in my head saying: 'Salvation once again, Mary.'

No bouncers came to throw me out when I got up on stage with Peter. I sang the jazz standard, 'All of Me', and I was astonished at the way he played the piano. I had never had accompaniment like it before. It was syncopated, like old ragtime records, and it fitted the style of my singing like a glove.

Peter was a wonderful, encouraging, talented, generous and lovably eccentric man. He was much older than me and jazz was his life. Through him, I got to know all the old jazzers in Dublin: guys who are in their eighties now and are still playing away.

Peter was the kind of man who would get an idea and see it right through to the end. He'd put up the posters, he'd get all the press and publicity, he'd approach the venue and he'd get everything sorted out and running smoothly.

He encouraged me to learn a lot of jazz standards – by

Bessie Smith, Ella Fitzgerald, Dinah Washington and my old favourite, Billie Holiday – telling me to put my own interpretation on them, the way I had done with 'Strange Fruit'. Then one day, he turned up at the door and said: 'We have a date in the National Concert Hall, just you and me: no other accompaniment.'

It was sold out overnight. Afterwards, fans were coming up to me and saying: 'My God, we never really *heard* you before, and with all the bands and all the electronics.' And they were right. Peter had a great feel for my phrasing, and there was a certain magic between us. He introduced me to the power in my own voice and it was a revelation.

Peter and I started to work regularly together, adding a double bass to the mix. We did gigs in England and Germany, and everyone loved this new departure. On one of our trips away, Peter and I were playing Ronnie Scott's in Birmingham, and there was a poster on the wall for a show where a woman was doing all the songs of Billie Holiday. Peter said: 'There's an idea. We could do that in Dublin.'

Years earlier, when I was sweeping the streets of London, I went to see a biopic of Billie Holiday starring Diana Ross, called *Lady Sings the Blues*. It was the first time I had ever heard of Holiday, and something about her story touched the heart of me. I went straight down to the Portobello Road after seeing the film, and bought all the Billie Holiday records I could find.

I recorded 'Good Morning Heartache' many years later, and 'Nobody's Business', as a kind of a nod to Billie. But record companies weren't interested and didn't want me to sing that kind of song: they didn't want to market me as a traditional jazz singer.

Right then, the timing couldn't have been better. A couple of weeks after Peter had his big idea, I was introduced to the promoter Pat Egan at a concert Frank and I attended. Pat told me he'd admired me as a singer for a long time, and knew all about the Big Cat/V2 debacle.

'What's going on with your music now?' he asked.

'Well, since you ask, I have a little project I'd love to talk to you about,' I replied.

One week later, Pat signed up to become the manager and promoter for our Billie Holiday show, which was to last another two years and would take me all over the world.

I knew everything about Billie. I could understand how her addiction utterly underpinned her singing: all the ups and downs she suffered in her short life echoed my own. Over the years, people had sent me cassettes and CDs of her work, comparing me to her, and when I was in the midst of my worst drinking binges, her rendition of 'Good Morning Heartache' was the dark song of my soul.

I think my connection to Billie Holiday's darkness and her downfall underpinned the show, and made it as successful as it was. Aoife had caught the Billie Holiday bug from me when she was a teenager, so she was thrilled to put the visuals together for the show. She got lots of photographs of Billie and some quotations, and projected them on a screen behind me. This contribution from Aoife, along with broadcaster John Kelly's narration, lent another layer of depth to the overall performance. People couldn't get enough of it.

From doing the show once or twice here and there, suddenly we were selling out six nights a week at a big venue in Dublin called HQ. We did ten weeks there and then moved to the Gaiety theatre for three nights, where the show sold out. After the performances, I would often meet people who had been to see it three or four times. There was a lot written about the show in the press across Europe, and in a small way I was back in the limelight again.

When we weren't doing long runs in Dublin, Peter and I did the bones of Billie Holiday here, there and everywhere with various sized bands, depending on what we could afford.

Cian had turned four and was starting school, and along with me working so hard, it was decided that we would get a new, live-in nanny. After looking through a few CVs from an agency, we eventually came upon Ana, a 25-year-old Spanish girl with tight, curly dark hair, who quickly became a fixture in the family. Ana was bright, bubbly and always smiling, and Clare and Cian followed her around like adoring little puppies. She was always painting with them or doing some sort of arts and crafts. There were jam jars everywhere in the house with paint brushes sticking out of them.

Ana came with me to lots of places, minding Cian when he wasn't at school, and became a friend and confidante to me.

As she had throughout my career, my mother kept every press clipping about the Billie Holiday show in a special scrapbook. In the previous few years, her health had deteriorated and by now she was more or less spending all of her days on the couch, unable and unwilling to get about, with my father looking after her every need. As always, we didn't know if she was really sick or not.

Since coming off the booze, I had wrestled long and hard with my confused feelings for my Mam. I was trying to come to terms with the fact that she had not protected me as a child and the way in which she had shut down any further talk of what happened to me when I told her the truth in the front room of our house, that day before I first went to London.

Looking back, I have often questioned why my mother was so emotionally removed. What happened to her in her own childhood that made it so hard for her to express love? Why was she so unable to handle the adoration we had for my father, and the love he had for his first three little girls? What was at the heart of the distance that lay between me and her, a distance neither of us could bridge? For my own part, I had been blaming her for a long, long time for everything that happened to me as a child, from the sexual abuse to the beatings from my Dad.

I had never invited my parents to stay in my house in Bray, but the Christmas after the Billie Holiday show had been recorded for a double album, I asked them up. I had come to the point of realising that they did the best they could. My father genuinely believed when he was beating us that he was doing it for our own good. It was the way he had been brought up himself, and he had apologised to me for it many times since I had grown up. There was no apology from my mother, but I had come to see that her actions – feeding me when I was lying prostrate in that hospital after the accident at Knocknacarra Cross, collecting clippings in that scrapbook, babysitting when my career first took off, being so good to my children – rather than her words, were her way of atoning. It was plain as the nose on my face that my mother loved the ground I walked on. I may not have been able to show her any love in return over the years, but I knew I had to let go of the guilt over that. I had done the best I could too. I couldn't possibly have been any other way.

When my parents were going home to Galway after the Christmas break, I drove them to Heuston Station. I had left them to the train many times in the past, but I had always said goodbye to them in the ticket hall. This time, I walked on to the platform, carrying their bags. I got on the train and made sure they had seats and then waited outside, looking in at them through the window, before the train moved off.

The whistle blew, and I was overcome with the feeling that I didn't want them to go. I put my palm on the window as the train began to move off. 'I love you,' I said to my mother, and I really meant it. Tears began to leak out the corners of her eyes. 'I love you too,' she said.

During one of my visits to Maura, she told me I had to stop beating myself up for the past so that I could move into a happier, healthier future.

Soon after, I met a man called Anthony Gorman, who was doing a workshop on a thing called Vortex Healing, which was something I could do myself at home on a daily basis. It's a kind a meditation using the energy of light. You lie down, relax your whole body and then start breathing light into the different chakra areas of your body. You can visualise the light as golden, violet or white: each colour represents a different kind of energy.

You work on the problems inside yourself, channelling light to help you to heal on physical, emotional and spiritual levels, all at the same time.

I got into Vortex Healing with a vengeance. I began to do weekend courses, learning all about it and spending time every night before I went to sleep, meditating with light. Although some people find the process hard to understand or believe, it began to help me. Maybe because, for the first time, I was taking the time to try and heal myself without the help of drink, drugs or other people. I was doing it for myself, by myself.

As I began to spiritually connect with myself, a nagging awareness that something was wrong in my house began to take root. I couldn't put my finger on it, but a lot of the bad feelings I had seemed to centre around the sitting room. To help change the energy, I redecorated the room from top to bottom, giving all the furniture to Eoin for his new house, but nothing worked. Part of me thought I was out of my mind, but another part of me was as logical as an accountant.

Then Frank asked me to marry him.

'What on God's green earth would we want to do a thing like that for?' I said. 'There's no need for it.'

But he kept asking and asking, wearing me down until I began to buckle.

'I have to do this for him,' I told myself. 'I've hurt him so badly over the years, and this will finally make up for it.'

I didn't feel one hundred percent sure about it, but I was sure that Frank loved me in his own way. I told myself it would work. We'd tie the knot and our relationship would grow and deepen: the wedding would bond us back together.

This, I convinced myself, was the next step on the right path. A couple of years earlier, Fintan had finally agreed to divorce me and there was nothing standing in my way. So eventually I said: 'Yes, Frank. I will marry you.'

We announced that we were getting married, and people were very happy for us. Carrie Crowley – who had a Sunday show on RTÉ Radio One, in which she interviewed people and got them to pick their favourite tunes – called Frank and asked him if he would be interested in going on the show to talk about his life.

At home, I tuned in and listened, as he waxed lyrical about his profound love for me, how much he had cared for me over the years, and how well suited we were to each other.

Carrie called me up afterwards and said: 'I've never met a man who loves anybody so much. You're a very lucky woman.'

We got engaged on my birthday, 5 May, just after I returned from doing the Billie Holiday show in Vienna. Frank went to the jewellers with Cian and picked out a beautiful diamond ring. That night I went up to Ana's room, and showed it off.

'Oh my God, it's absolutely gorgeous,' she said, her eyes wet with emotion.

I skipped back downstairs, full of the joys of spring. As I would discover much later, Ana then went into the toilet and puked her guts up.

She had been having an affair with Frank, shagging him on the sofa in our sitting room while I was out working. A few weeks before the wedding, Ana suddenly quit, saying she was going to do some college course or other. Suspecting nothing, I was desperately sad to see her go.

19

'I've Grown Accustomed to His Face'

The first time I went to America to visit Frank, at the beginning of our relationship, he suggested one evening that we play 'trust games'. These are little exercises people do as part of group therapy to instill a sense of faith in each other. In one of them, you hold your own fist up to your face and the other person pulls it back slowly, using a lot of force. If they let go, your arm will spring back and you'll thump yourself in the face. I was reluctant to play, but Frank insisted: 'I'm not going to let go. I promise. I'm not going to let go.'

He did let go, and I whacked myself hard between the eyes. One of my eyes went black and my nose started gushing blood. I said to myself there and then: 'Here you go again, Mary, you bloody eejit, falling for the wrong man.'

Ever since that moment, a little voice inside regularly told me that I couldn't trust Frank, but I never listened to a word it said. Now, in the lead-up to the wedding, that little voice was getting louder and louder. Still, I continued to ignore it.

The big day was planned for 11 September 2002, a year after

the attack on the twin towers. One of Frank's favourite songs was 'I've Grown Accustomed to Her Face', from the musical *My Fair Lady*. I learned the lyrics and practiced my own version of it, replacing 'her' with 'his', the way Peggy Lee did. Peter was accompanying me on the piano. It was going to be my little surprise for Frank, after the speeches were done.

In typical fashion, I said: 'Well, fuck it. If I'm going to have a wedding, I'm going to do it big.' I decided to invite everyone in the world we knew. Endless lists were made, endless seating plans. I became completely caught up in the whole thing, going over to Australia and New Zealand in the midst of it all to do Billie Holiday gigs. I was really beginning to build fan bases in both countries.

I got myself into shape, power-walking and starving myself, so I could fit into the dress Claire Garvey had designed for me. The venue was booked: Glendalough House in Wicklow. There would be a marquee outside. Three hundred invitations had gone off in the post and the RSVPs were beginning to flood in.

Frank and Neil decided to go away on a stag weekend.

'Do you think we should have a last fling before we get married?' Frank asked me before he went.

I couldn't believe my ears. 'You want to shag someone else?' I said.

'I don't know,' he replied. 'Maybe. Do you?'

I told him I could never do that. If I went with someone else, it would mean the end for us, and he knew it.

'You're right,' he said. 'I love you. See you in a few days.'

The little voice inside me shouted out a warning, but I told it to shut up.

*

The day before the wedding, I went down to the Kilcoole Farmer's Market, where they always sold wild flowers. I had told them in advance that I wanted to buy all the flowers that Saturday, so that I could arrange them myself. I piled them into a van and drove up to Glendalough to do bunches on each of the tables in the marquee.

Frank's mother was over from America, along with his brother. Mammy and Daddy were up from Galway, booked into the Michael Collins room, which tickled my father pink. Mammy wasn't well at all. She had been in and out of hospital a few times. She was very tense about everything and not fully able to enjoy herself.

Daddy, on the other hand, was like a child, going around filming everything with the video camera I had given him the previous Christmas.

We got married in the courthouse in Wicklow town. Arriving in the limo, I got a fit of the giggles and had to try to smother them. Half the nation's newspaper photographers were waiting for me when I stepped out of the car.

Before we went in, I said to someone: 'Give me a cigarette.' I didn't smoke at all, but in that moment, I needed something. A photograph of me in my dress, puffing away on a fag behind a pillar, appeared in the papers the next day. I looked like a criminal about to be handed a sentence.

Catherine Geraghty – the bridesmaid Mammy wouldn't let me have at my first wedding – was given the job this time around, and she helped at every little step. Neil was Frank's best man. My children were all dressed up to the nines, with happy smiles lighting up their faces, Cian the only guest in a tux, because he wanted to look like James Bond.

Later on, after the meal and the speeches, Brian Kennedy sang the Van Morrison song, 'Have I Told You Lately that I Love You?' for the bride and groom's first dance. Frank whispered in my ear as he led me around the floor: 'Thank you for doing this. You have made me so incredibly happy and I really, really love you.'

Not ten feet away, sitting at a table on the edge of the floor, Ana watched us dance.

When I sat down, Peter came over and said: 'Well, Mary, it's now or never.' It was time for me to sing 'I've Grown Accustomed to His Face', to surprise my new husband.

The little voice inside said: 'Don't do it,' and this time, for some unknown reason, I listened. 'You know what?' I said to Peter, 'I don't think I want to sing at all today. Let's leave it.'

I grew to be very glad that I never sang that song. It would have been the most bitter of humiliations.

Ken Livingston invited me to perform at the St Patrick's Day open-air concert in London the following March. Frank, who hadn't been to a gig in about five years, said he would like to come along. The night before the concert there was a big reception at the Dorchester, so we booked a room. All the Irish high-flyers were there: people like Bob Geldof, Ronnie Drew, The Fureys and Diarmuid Gavin. It was a big celebration of Irish celebrity.

Eventually, as it often does since I stopped drinking, the night got a bit boring. Everyone at my table, bar me, was absolutely scuttered on free drink, so I excused myself and went off to bed.

At about three in the morning, Frank stumbled into our room, sat on the bed and gave me a nudge to wake up.

'Leave me alone Frank, will you?' I said. 'I have to be at a soundcheck in a few hours.'

'I have to talk to you,' he said. He turned on the lights, sat back down again and blurted out: 'I've had an affair.'

You can bet your life I was wide awake then. I started shouting and bawling and roaring so loud, I'd say the whole of the Dorchester could hear me. 'Who is it?' I screamed. 'Who are you fucking, Frank?'

He told me he had had two affairs in the past couple of years, while on business trips to America. I cried so hard that by the time I had to get a taxi down to the London Eye, where the St Patrick's Day concert stage was rigged up, my eyes were like two big red puffballs.

'You poor thing,' my agent, Susie, said when she saw me. 'What are you going to do?'

My jaw hit the ground. Had Frank broadcast his infidelities to all and sundry the previous evening before coming upstairs to inform me?

'Vince Power is on his way down,' said Susie.

'Oh, sweet Jesus, Vince knows,' I thought. 'Who else knows? Are they all going around saying what a stupid fucking moron Mary's been?' Everything started to go in slow motion.

'We're trying to contact the police,' Susie said and I was like: 'What the fuck? Are they going to arrest Frank for sleeping around?'

It turned out that my piano player had been involved in a fracas in the Dorchester the night before. He'd been on the dry for ages, but he'd hit the free whiskey big time and gotten out of his tree. The police had carted him off to the station, and he was locked up.

At that moment, this news was almost worse than everyone knowing about Frank. I was getting paid a lot of money to do this gig. There were 75,000 people assembling in front of the stage as we spoke.

Frank turned up, his tail between his legs. He knew about the piano player and said: 'We'll sort something out, don't worry.'

I told him to fuck off and get out of my sight.

I figured I could sing 'Seduced' on my own, and do my a cappella version of 'Strange Fruit', but that was hardly going to fill my twenty-minute slot. One of The Dubliners said he'd try to play along with a few songs on his guitar.

Eventually Frank came back and said: 'I've found Brian Connor.'

Brian was over in London to play with Eleanor McEvoy. We rehearsed the set quickly, changing a few songs to fit in with what Brian was familiar with from working with me before. On stage, I got through my twenty minutes, smiling for the audience and cracking a few jokes, all the time knowing Frank was out there watching me.

We were booked to stay another night at the Dorchester, but I packed my bags and we went back to Ireland the minute the gig was finished. I cried all the way to the airport and when I got home, I got into my bed and cried for another two days.

The night after we came home, Frank started begging for forgiveness, telling me he was so sorry for hurting me. At first I told him he should leave then and there.

'I'm going to use this as a stick to beat you with for the rest of your life,' I warned him.

He said he knew I had every right never to speak to him again, but for the sake of the kids, and for the sake of our love, which had been proven by the fact that he had stayed with me through all the years, we had to try to get over this. He said that he had always suspected I was sleeping around myself, when I was drinking and on the road. This is something I never, ever did, but somehow, without me noticing it, the tables began to turn. I was becoming the one to blame for what had happened.

'Look at him,' I thought. 'He's in bits. I've really fucked this man up.'

So I agreed to try and work it out with him. Nobody knew a thing about it: his affairs had taken place in America. They had been out of sight, and maybe I could put them out of mind. If I could forgive him, and accept that I had played my part, we could put this behind us. We were quits now. I had hurt him badly; he had hurt me in return. The playing field was even.

About two weeks later, as Frank and I were having breakfast before he went out to work, he said: 'As long as we're being honest with each other, I have something else to tell you. I had an affair with Ana.'

I went into such a state of rage that I could have easily beaten him to death there and then. Ana had lived with us for three years. I adored her. She was the best carer I ever had had for my kids. She had done everything for them, had acted as my friend and confidante, and she had been sleeping with my husband behind my back.

'Get the fuck out of this house and never come back!' I screamed at Frank.

He put his hand on his heart and said: 'It will never happen again. You have to believe me.'

But how could I believe him? How could I ever trust him again?

I didn't know what to do. Who to tell. Where to turn. Everyone would be laughing at me. The man I had married had been sleeping with the nanny just before he walked up the aisle with me. I turned it all in on myself, and repeated the old mantra: 'It's all your fault, Mary. All your fault. How could you have driven this man to do such a terrible thing?'

I tracked down Ana, and made her come to the house. I got the two of them into the kitchen and marched up and down, saying: 'Tell me everything, or so help me God, I'll murder both of you.'

I forced them to tell me every sordid detail of what they had done together: the times; the places; everything. It's something I wish I hadn't done, because sometimes I'm still haunted by visions of them having sex.

When I was three years sober, I was awarded a gold medal from the Rutland Centre. On it was written: 'I am responsible'. The awards ceremony in Milltown was a big occasion for all the ex-clients who had stayed sober for three years, and their families, with more than a thousand people at it.

Clare was five at the time I got my medal, and Frank brought her to the ceremony.

I had a speech to do and I was a bag of nerves, even though I was used to being in front of people. It meant so much to me to get this medal. I had made my speech notes, in which I wanted to give thanks to Frank for staying with me through the worst of it all. I went up to the podium with everyone clapping and cheering, and as I began to speak, I saw that Frank was walking out the door with Clare.

I had asked him why he left, and he told me that Clare had needed to go to the bathroom, which I fully accepted. The medal said, 'I am responsible.' It was the moment in my life in which I separated myself from him, stopped being dependent on him.

I knew it was never going to be OK. I knew I was endangering my sobriety and my sanity for a pretence of a relationship. I knew that I had to sort it out, *now*. I went home and sat Frank down. 'Okay, here's the deal,' I said. 'Get yourself a good therapist, sort your head out and then we'll get some marriage counselling. We'll give it a go.'

He got a counsellor from the *Golden Pages*, who told him he should take up golf and start feeling better about himself.

Aoife announced her engagement to her partner, James. It was clear to me that he was a man who was committed to her happiness – good and loving husband material – so I was delighted for her. The wedding would take place in Rome in September, with a party at our house in Bray two weeks later. I decided to have the whole house redecorated for the wedding party, with new bathrooms and a new kitchen put in. Still thinking Frank was going to therapy, I threw myself into the preparations. We had plenty of money to splash about, and I thought: 'Why not?' I was trying to fix everything again.

I organised the whole wedding to within an inch of its life, before taking off at the beginning of June for Australia to do the Billie Holiday show again. Ollie was living in Sydney by now, with her partner, Damien. Cian and Clare were getting school holidays, so I took them with me. Ollie hadn't seen them in two years.

We all booked into a hotel in the Blue Mountains outside Sydney, and I felt more relaxed than I had been for ages. There was a palpable sense of relief in the children too and we were all having a lovely time. Sitting in my hotel room, as Clare tried on Ollie's clothes, with the two of them laughing away, and Cian giggling on the bed with me, I realised that I could do this on my own. If I left Frank, it wouldn't destroy my family.

The next morning, I got up before dawn and walked to the edge of town to look at the sunrise over the mountains. Sitting there, watching the sky light up orange then a crystal-clear blue, with the smell of eucalyptus all around me, I felt a sense of peace and strength that was completely new. My medal from the Rutland Centre said, 'I am responsible'. I suddenly understood on a deep level, not only in my head, but in my heart, that the responsibility was to myself.

'I am responsible for myself,' I said out loud. 'I am responsible for myself.'

I went back to the hotel and e-mailed Frank. 'We're finished,' I wrote. 'Over and done with. I don't want this anymore.'

I told Ollie about the e-mail. She said: 'Mam, Frank loves you. Everybody knows Frank loves you.'

Everybody knew but me. I never felt it.

Before I left for Australia, Mammy had been in and out of hospital. She had had a stent put in while I was away, but when she got home something happened and she had to be re-admitted to Galway Regional. I went to see her when I got back.

The doctor had told Mammy she would be dancing with my father at Aoife's wedding, the way the two of them had danced at the Warwick Hotel when they were first courting. She was looking forward to it. Her sister Vera was coming over, Daddy was all lined up with his video camera, and as far as they knew, it was all rosy in the garden. I hadn't said a word about Frank.

She got out of the hospital about a week before the wedding, but Dad phoned me to say that none of them were coming after all. Mam was feeling awful and she didn't want him or Vera at the wedding if she couldn't go. They had to stay home and take care of her.

'Put her on to me,' I said. Mammy had been feeling awful for twenty bloody years. Nobody really knew whether she was really sick, or whether she was putting it on.

I told her to snap out of it, and that I would never forgive her if she stopped my father from coming to his Aoife's wedding, not to mention Vera, who had travelled all the way from America. 'Stop being so selfish for once in your life,' I said.

Later on, Dad called me up and said: 'Mary, you'd better apologise to your mother for what you said. You'll regret it for the rest of your life if you don't.'

I would realise later that poor Mammy was in an awful state: in terrible pain and afraid for her life.

We had a lovely few days in Rome for the actual ceremony itself. It was a wonderful family time, with Frank making big gestures by taking everyone to lunch every day. I knew he was hurting. I knew that he knew it was finished.

We decided on a Moroccan theme for the party at home, and Ollie built a kasbah in the front porch of the house, with loads of cushions and a big carpet. There were a thousand candles all over the house in little red jars: Cian and Clare went around lighting them at sunset.

Fintan came to give Aoife away: she had invited him to be there. After the speeches, she sang 'The First Time Ever I Saw Your Face' for James. I looked over and saw that Frank was crying. In that moment, my heart went out to him. The beginning of my daughter's married life was coinciding with the end of ours.

Mammy passed away six weeks later. It transpired that the stent they put in had taken away a piece of her artery, and it had migrated into her kidneys. She had endured an agonising six or seven weeks, all swollen up with fluid. When I went to see her after the wedding, she looked like a different person.

The next few weeks were unbearable. To be fair to him, Frank was very on-the-ball. He had a lot of medical knowledge about what was going on and spoke to doctors on our behalf, accompanying me on lots of the trips up and down to Galway, as Mammy deteriorated.

Sometimes she'd open her eyes and you knew she wanted to speak, but nothing would come out. They put her into a coma for a few days and gave her some dialysis to make her comfortable, but her lungs filled up with fluid and her heart couldn't pump without life support.

Daddy said she never wanted to end up with a machine keeping her alive. He wanted to turn it off, and after talking about it, we all agreed it was the best thing. Then my brother Gerard, who had never been one for outward displays of emotion, said: 'Leave her alone, she's fine, she's going to get better.'

Over the next few days, one by one, we went in to talk to our mother alone. When it was my turn, I took her hand and said: 'I'm sorry for all the pain I caused over the years, Mammy. You know I love you, don't you?'

Her eyes were open and she was looking directly at me. I think she heard every word.

Mammy passed away peacefully, surrounded by all of us. It wasn't what I expected it to be. All the weeping and wailing had been done, and the moment she left us, there was a palpable feeling of release in the room. It was like someone who had been holding their breath for a long, painful time had just let go and breathed it all out. I breathed out with her, knowing that I would never see her alive again, but that she had gone to a better place.

As I drove out with her in the hearse to Claregalway for her removal, I realised that it was now or never. I had to embrace my own life. I had to leave Frank. When it was my turn to die, I wanted to know that I had lived to the best of my ability by honouring myself and my family. I wanted to stop being angry at myself and come to the point where my children weren't angry with me anymore. I wanted to let go of guilt.

We had Mammy laid out at home for two days, and then we faced into the funeral. Before she went to the church, we wanted to walk behind the hearse through Shantalla. Hundreds of people were out on the street, dropping to their knees as the coffin went by. When we came up Ashe Road, every one of the neighbours came out onto the street and followed the coffin up to the church.

Mammy was buried beside Valerie, my sister who had died at birth. As she went into the ground and my father sobbed beside me, I said to myself: 'I am going to live to the best of my ability for every single day that's left to me.'

20

'Antarctica'

While we were in Rome for Aoife's wedding, I spotted a beautiful glass chandelier in an antique shop, but it was broken. I have always loved old glass chandeliers: the way their hanging pendants disperse light throughout a room. I bought this one, and I dragged the parts of it on board the plane home in plastic bags. When we got back to Ireland, my friend Mag gave me lots of extra crystals to hang on it. She cleaned the chandelier with methylated spirits and we hung it in the sitting room of the house in Bray.

To me, that chandelier was a symbol of all the love, care and attention I had put into No. 2 Martello Terrace. Piece by piece, I had slowly restored that house to its former glory, and it was the only tangible thing I had to show for all my years of hard work, all the ups and downs of my career.

In the months following my mother's funeral, the house became a bone of contention between Frank and me. Our marriage was finished, as far as I was concerned. I wanted him gone, but he had no intention of leaving.

As Christmas approached, we veered between screaming matches to not speaking to each other at all for days on end. We both dug our heels in, each of us as immovable as stone. I hated him with a bitter vengeance, so much so that I could hardly bear to look at his face.

That's not to say that I wasn't hugely sad as well. Deep down, I really did still have love for Frank, despite his betrayal. There was a time when I would have nearly laid down my life for him, and, although we move on in our lives, I don't think those feelings ever go away fully. Somewhere in our bodies, our hearts or our minds, we hold on to the things we once cherished about the people we loved. We don't have to be with them anymore, we don't even have to fully like them anymore, but the memory of love is always there.

Neil's new film, *The Good Thief*, was being premiered in Dublin. It would be one of the last events Frank and I attended together. It was a heist movie starring Nick Nolte, and featured lots of fantastic reproductions of paintings by the masters of modern art as part of the props. After the screening, there was a party in Lillie's Bordello, where the paintings were auctioned off for charity. One of them was a beautiful version of a Modigliani nude, with every brushstroke spot on. I couldn't take my eyes off it.

Before the auction started, I clocked Denis Desmond sitting with a group of his friends. I waved at him, and he beckoned me over. 'How have you been, Mary?' he asked.

'I've never been better,' I said.

As we chatted about this and that for a few minutes, I

realised that all my anger towards Denis was gone. I had let it go without even realising.

As the night wound down and the auction was finished, a woman came over to me, carrying the 'Modigliani'. 'It's yours,' she said, handing it to me. 'Mr Desmond bought it for you.'

I was hanging fairy lights out in the porch one afternoon, trying to look forward to Christmas in the house with Frank, when I saw a black woman walk past the gate carrying a suitcase. I waved hello at her and she asked if I knew any B & Bs in the area. She had just arrived in Bray from Zimbabwe to take up a job in a hotel up the road. Her name was Pretty, and she had big white smile that stretched from one ear to the other.

'Do you want to come and live here?' I said.

Pretty moved in, and it was as if God had sent down an angel. When Frank arrived back that evening, she was already part of the furniture. The children took to her immediately, and her presence in our house was a soothing balm, even though the undercurrents of anger still ran strong.

Just before Christmas, I received an e-mail from the Christchurch Jazz Festival in New Zealand, asking me if I would come and do the Billie Holiday show there in February. Although it meant I would have to leave the children for a few weeks, I jumped at the chance. Pretty would look after them, and I wouldn't be gone for too long.

For years, two of my long-time friends, Angie and Rosie, were always giving out before I went off halfway across the world to do gigs. 'We wish you'd take us with you,' they'd say. 'We could be your backing singers.'

This time I said to them: 'Why don't you come? We'll manage it financially, one way or the other.' Within about three minutes, Rosie won €4,000 on the lotto, so we decided the trip was meant to be. The tickets were bought, the suitcases were packed and the three of us headed off into the sunset.

When we landed in Christchurch, we were met by Marianne Hargreaves, who was running the festival, and her friend Jodi Wright. They brought us to a beautiful apartment in the Arts Centre that would be our home for the next few weeks.

The plan was that I would do the Billie Holiday show for four nights running in the Town Hall, which was the main venue for the Festival, and then finish up with one night doing my own material in the Great Hall at the Arts Centre. Because I was working with a new band, there was a week of rehearsals to get through beforehand. Angie and Rosie decided to rent a car and take off for a bit of travelling while I got my act together.

On the first day of rehearsals, a guy came up to me and started discussing the lighting for the gig. He was worried about the visuals that Aoife had put together for the show, which I had brought with me on disc.

'Listen,' I said, 'I don't give a fuck about the lights.'

He turned around and walked across the theatre to the lighting desk, and looking at him, I got a very strange feeling: something I recognised, but couldn't put my finger on.

Before the end of the week, I had completely fallen for this man. I was like a teenage girl with her first crush. His name was John Kelly, and he had long blond hair and twinkly blue eyes. He was a silent little creature who would hardly even look at me, but I was infatuated beyond all measure.

I had not felt sexually aroused for years, not in the slightest bit attracted to anyone. Love was bullshit as far as I was concerned: men were arseholes. I was never going to be hurt again. I'd be on my own from now on, and that was that. If I wanted a bit of sexual relief, I figured I'd have to investigate the joys of a vibrator.

And suddenly, here I was, moon-eyed like a little lamb over a much younger guy, a guy who didn't seem to even notice me. 'Sweet Mother of Divine Jesus Christ Almighty, stop it!' I castigated myself. 'He's only a young fella. You're forty-seven: old and past it. He wouldn't have a bit of a heed on you.'

The night of the first concert, Jodi's daughter, Chelsea, who is a make-up artist, came into my dressing room to get me together. I had lovely gowns for the show, and my hair and make-up were to be done in a perfect 1950s style. I started quizzing her about John as she got to work.

'Well, he's worked for us for fourteen years,' she said. 'I couldn't tell you what age he is. I don't know where he lives. I don't know if he's gay or straight, or married or divorced, but I can tell you one thing: he is one of the most genuine guys I have ever met.'

Angie and Rosie had come back from their travels and this girly thing started up between us, me telling them about fancying John, them figuring out how to get us together. But it was all joking around. I knew I didn't have a snowball's chance in hell of ever being with him.

On the last night of the Billie Holiday shows, John came up to me and said: 'Sorry, Mary, I can't do the lighting for your own show tomorrow night. I have to work on another gig.'

'No worries,' I said. 'You did an amazing job, and thank you very much.'

He drove me back to my flat and planted a kiss on my cheek. 'It was wonderful working with you Mary,' he said, and maybe we'll meet again.' That night I went back to my room alone, and stayed up crying until dawn. I was absolutely sure and positive that I would never know what it was like to kiss anybody again in my life. Before John came along, I hadn't even missed it, but now I realised I was starved of love and intimacy.

As morning dawned, there was no coffee in the room, but I knew a little place called Le Café that opened at 6.30 a.m. Red-eyed and wrecked, I went out and got myself a take-away coffee. As I sat on the steps, sipping it, the sound engineer from the gigs, Simon, came along.

'What's wrong?' he asked, sitting down beside me.

'I think my life is over, Simon,' I said. 'I really like this guy and he doesn't even know that I exist.'

He said: 'Why don't you tell him?'

That night, as I was getting ready to go on stage, Chelsea came into my dressing room and said: 'John's here. He got somebody else to do the other gig, and he's down in the back with Simon.'

Although I couldn't see him, every single song I sang that night, I sang for John.

When we were packing up, he came to me and said: 'We're all going to the Festival Club. Are you coming?'

Later, when we were there, he asked: 'Would you like to go for a drive?' And so I found myself sitting in his truck, driving along the Port Hills, looking down over Christchurch, with its beautiful harbour surrounded by still, dark water reflecting the moon.

John told me that when he was a student, he had heard a song on college radio called 'Little Death'. He had never forgotten it, and it wasn't until he heard me rehearsing it that he put two and two together and realised it was me.

He asked me if I wanted to get out of the truck to look at the city lights. By the time we got back in the truck, the two of us were in a daze. Driving past the Servo station, John stopped and said: 'I'll get us some protection.'

'No way,' I laughed. I couldn't imagine having sex with anybody, much less this beautiful young man. 'Thanks very much for the kiss,' I said. 'I'll go away and die happy now.'

Two days later, we were still in bed.

I am convinced that my mother sent John to me. The first night we spent together was her birthday.

Angie and Rosie cautioned me not to tell Frank about John. 'You'll lose everything,' they said. I, on the other hand, thought honesty would be the best policy. I had a fairytale notion, whereby Frank would accept it, we'd sort out our affairs and we'd both go our separate ways. Nothing could have prepared me for his reaction when he found out.

The minute I walked into the house, he guessed.

'You've met a man,' he said, and I couldn't deny it. It was the truth.

He flew into a rage, every bit of anger and resentment he'd

held inside for years erupting out of him like a volcano. He called me every name under the sun, screaming at me to get out of the house, and telling me I would never see the children again.

That night, while I slept, Frank got my phone, found texts from John and rang him.

'That's my wife you're fucking,' he said. 'If you ever ring this number again, I will come over there and break both your arms.'

He told John that I was a coke addict and an alcoholic, that I'd done this before, and that I treated men as playthings.

'That's not the Mary I know,' John said, but after weeks of texts and daily phone calls from him, there wasn't a peep out of my phone for the next three days. I had no idea Frank had spoken to him. I just figured John had lost all interest.

Then Frank told me. 'You won't be hearing from lover boy again,' he said. 'I told him everything about you. I told him you were a mess, that you messed people's lives up because you're so fucked-up. I told him to steer well clear of you.'

Later that night I found a bag of coke in the house and horsed into it. The next day, I pulled myself together and phoned the Rutland Centre. I told Maura what I had done and about everything that had happened. I said to her that I never wanted to take cocaine again. During that month in New Zealand, I had had a glimpse of what could be: I wanted to stop for once and for all. Maura arranged for me to do a re-entry programme which took place once a week over the next six weeks.

I called John and said to him: 'I told you from the start I was a drug addict and an alcoholic. But I am not a slut. There's never been anybody else since the day I met Frank.'

And then John said the words I thought I would never hear in my lifetime: 'I believe you, Mary.'

John Kelly believed in me. Up to that point, absolutely nobody in my life – apart from counsellors and therapists who are paid to do their jobs – had believed in me. Least of all myself.

John had gone to Jodi, who knew me very well, and told her about what Frank had said. She told him: 'You've got to know that if you're getting involved with this woman, anything can happen. She could slip with drugs or alcohol again. If you want to do this, you better hold on tight because you're in for the ride of your life.'

On the phone he said: 'If you want to do this, Mary, I'm in for the long haul.'

In the meantime, Frank told everyone that Mary was leaving him for a toy boy in New Zealand. I told him: 'I'm not going any-where. You're the one getting out of this house, and that's that.'

But as time went on, we were still at loggerheads and Frank wasn't going anywhere.

One Saturday afternoon, when he was away for a weekend, I was in a queue at the supermarket, buying stuff to make a special Mexican dinner for the kids. Two women, who had once been on a trip to Lourdes with Mammy, came up to me and said: 'How's your mother, Mary?'

I broke down and started wailing. I ran out of the supermarket, leaving the trolley and the two women high and dry.

At home I paced the kitchen like a lunatic, crying and begging my mother to help me. 'If you can do anything, do it now,' I said. 'You weren't able to help me when you were alive. Get the fucking finger out now!'

A knock came on the door, and standing there was the artist Brian Bourke from Galway, who I hadn't seen since the night of my going-away party, when I was arrested for drink-driving so many years ago. Brian had met Ollie in the town, and she had told him what was going on.

He sat in the kitchen and I poured out my heart and soul to him. He said: 'Jesus, Mary, I was just talking to Helen Quinn, and she was going on about how happy you and Frank were.'

Helen had been at our wedding, and had said it was one of the best days out she ever had.

'I'll give her a shout and she'll come over,' said Brian. 'She'll know what to do.'

Helen came and listened to my story. 'Pack your bags, Mary,' she said. 'It's time to get out and I know exactly where you can go.'

She took a set of keys out of her bag and explained that her daughter Hannah and her husband Tim had gone away to make a movie, and that their flat would be empty for nine months. 'It's yours if you want it,' she said.

I silently thanked my mother for her intervention, and as I did, a photograph of her that was stuck to the fridge with a magnet, fell on to the ground. I picked it up, knowing she was with me. That photograph would come with me to my new home.

It was a stunningly beautiful, luxurious flat, and I did my

best to make a home for the kids there, but much of the time they wanted to be in the house with Frank. I struggled with this for months, but slowly I began to realise that I would have to accept it. I would have to be a mother to them in the best way I could, without trying to control their choices. If I was lonely, it wasn't their responsibility.

I was on the phone to Erik's ex-wife one evening and I told her everything that had happened over the past few years, about my difficulties with Frank. She told me about a song she had written once when she was in Christchurch, New Zealand: 'Antarctica'. She quoted bits of it and I thought, now that's a song for me.

There had been no contact between me and Erik since *After The Fall*, six years earlier. I e-mailed him and said: 'I've had the worst year of my life, and I need to be moving on. I need to start work on a new album and I can't do it without you.'

'Where do you want to do it?' he asked.

'New Zealand,' I replied, quick as a flash, and he said: 'No problem.'

I went for six weeks, and we worked really hard every single day with a piano player called Tom Rainey. I had a few songs that I already knew I wanted to include. One of them was my own, a song called 'Mary, Mary', about the time I threw myself on the ground when I was a tiny little girl, kicking the buckles off my brand new shoes because I was so frightened of my uncle. Another was a song by Kristina Olsen, called 'In My Darkened Room', which brought me back to all those nights drinking with just a mattress and a ghetto blaster playing Billie Holiday. Angela McCluskey's song, 'Sleep On It', told of the many years when I allowed myself to stay in the wrong situations because I believed I had made my bed and now I had to lie on it.

Erik and I worked on about twenty-five songs, which we needed to whittle down to thirteen. We had bridged a gap, and come together to make our best music yet. Denis had agreed to finance the album when it was done, without blinking an eye, so in a strange way, we had all come full circle.

Every evening I went home to John, who held me through the sad moments and laughed with me late into the night.

I knew that when we finished work on the album I would have to go back to Ireland to face into the often lonely life I had chosen for myself, away from my children and still not properly talking to Frank.

'I'm coming to Ireland with you, Mary,' John said on my last day.

'You can't,' I said. 'You don't know what you're letting yourself in for.'

'Neither do you,' he said.

Never a truer word was spoken.

Epilogue

25 April 2009

'The House of the Rising Sun'

It's Sunday afternoon. I'm in the kitchen cooking lunch. John is sitting at the breakfast counter, chatting to Ollie's partner, Damien, and Aoife's husband, James. It's hard to believe, but John and I have been together for four years. And counting.

Ollie has moved into the house next door with Damien. She's always in and out, borrowing this or that, chatting over cups of coffee. Clare and Cian are in the big white sitting room, lying on the couches, watching a Harry Potter DVD. Cian's hair has a streak of blue in it, the beginnings of a teenager striking out on his own.

Eoin, who lives a few doors up the road, arrives and surveys the array of food in the kitchen. He's back at college now, studying science, and he's always starving.

Running from room to room, tormenting our dog, Billie, is my granddaughter, Meíni. Her mother, Aoife, is helping me in the kitchen. She's pregnant again, expecting in three months.

The day Aoife first asked me to come over and babysit for

my granddaughter was very special for me. It meant so much that she trusted me enough to look after her precious baby.

I'm only now trying to be the mother all my children deserved, giving them the respect and freedom and nurturing they are entitled to.

They have each had their difficulties, difficulties that have roots in my own past behaviour and life. But, by and large, they are doing well. They are the next generation of my family. As part of my own generation, I have made my own journey towards being a healthy person, trying to live to the best of my ability. I am still making that journey. From my grandparents, to my parents, to myself, we are all part of the same journey.

In January, my father turned eighty. He organised his own huge party in a hotel in Galway for the occasion, and the entire family came. After dinner, myself, Angela and Carol got up on the stage and belted out our party piece, 'The House of the Rising Sun'. We were his three girls again that night, and I have never seen him happier.

Even though it's been almost five years since Mammy died, he still misses her desperately. He visits her grave every day and makes sure it's looking lovely.

It's Cian's confirmation next week. I have asked Frank to come to the house that day and he's said yes.

Erik and I are planning to do another album. 'Maybe we should make this one a little happier,' he says, but I'm still attracted to the dark songs. That will probably always be the same with me, no matter how much more in control of my life I am.

My last album, *The House of Ill Repute*, didn't sell so well in

Ireland, which was disappointing to me, because you always want to be accepted on your own turf. It got good reviews across the board in England, and was voted one of the top twelve albums of the year in Germany in 2008. On the back of this, I've got a new manager, Paul Loasby, and I'm booked for a tour of England, Finland, Denmark, Sweden and Norway at the end of 2009. In the meantime, I will be playing the Sydney Opera House and touring other parts of Australia and New Zealand in the summer. My gigs in Christchurch, New Zealand, are already sold out.

Boxed away upstairs, I have photographs of myself being pushed around on a trolley in an airport in Finland, drinking a bottle of vodka with a straw, the word 'ALCO' written in capitals in blue marker on the bottle's label, and a 'Fragile' sticker plastered to my forehead.

Maybe I wasn't so fragile after all. Here I am, surrounded by my family and a long time free of the drugs and alcohol that plagued my life for so long.

I'm singing again, some of the best material I've ever performed, and gigging all over the place. But the most exciting things are getting up every morning and making breakfast with my kids, or getting into my car to go over to Aoife's house to see my granddaughter.

I am not a little girl inside anymore. I have taken so many steps in the past few years to become a responsible adult, responsible for myself, and I'm never going back.

ACKNOWLEDGEMENTS

A big thank you to all of the musicians and songwriters I've worked with through my years in the music business, far too many to mention by name but they know who they are. And to Denis and Vince.

A very special thanks to Erik Visser, for everything.

I would like to thank my children, Aoife, Olwen, Eoin, Clare and Cian, and all the other members of my family, most especially my father, my sisters Angela and Carol, my brothers Ger and Martin, my many nephews and nieces and all of my extended family.

Big thanks to my partner John, literally the light of my life.

To Maura Russell, Susan Eustace, Declan.

To my many friends who have stuck with me through thick and thin over the years – you know who you are. Special thanks to John and Cindy, Catherine and Johnny, Angie and Rosie, Mag, Norma and Pretty. To Jodi and Mez in New Zealand and all my friends and family there.

Many thanks to Brian Finnegan for all his help with the writing of this book, and to my editor Ciara Considine and all at Hachette Books Ireland.